Shackled and Chained

Mass Incarceration in Capitalist America

PSL PUBLICATIONS

SAN FRANCISCO

ISBN: 978-0-9841220-8-0
Library of Congress Control Number: 2013910887
Printed in the United States

Written by

Eugene Puryear

Editors

Ben Becker, Jon Britton

Staff

Meghann Adams, Anne Gamboni, Saul Kanowitz,
Gloria La Riva, Mazda Majidi, Keith Pavlik

PSL Publications

2969 Mission Street #201
San Francisco, CA 94110
(415) 821-6171
books@PSLweb.org
www.PSLweb.org

Shackled and Chained

Introduction

PRISONS and prison issues touch some of society's rawest nerves. To end up in prison, in jail or on parole or probation means that one has transgressed against the legal code—committed a "crime." Legal codes, however, are not made up of timeless principles. Rather, they are constructed to conform to the interests of a particular set of people—the dominant class—across a particular period of time.

For instance, in the United States interracial marriage was once illegal in any number of states. Slavery—outside of prison—was also legal for an extended period, just as it was illegal for women to vote. There are humorous publications that detail the numerous inane laws that remain on the books but are not enforced because of their anti- quated character—the broader point being what is and is not a crime can be quite relative.

Even when there is a broad consensus about the criminality of certain actions, there are extensive discussions about how to best deal with such infractions, both after the fact and preventively.

This book attempts to engage with these issues in the contem- porary American context. As the title suggests, we situate the current criminal justice policies of the United States in the context of capitalism, and more particularly the socio-economic realities of roughly the last 40 years. We do this not merely because this is the system we live under, but because the exigencies of this period and their impact on the capital- ist class decisively shaped our modern system of crime and punishment.

Using this as our general thesis, this study is divided into three basic sections. First, we examine the demographics of the prison pop- ulation and the conditions in which inmates live. We outline these broad trends at the start of our narrative, because without understand- ing who is imprisoned and in what percentages it becomes impossible to construct a coherent narrative separating cause from effect.

Our second section goes into the historical background of U.S. imprisonment, beginning with a brief history of prisons in the United States. We then trace in detail the historical factors of the last 40 years with the most direct bearing on the massive explosion of the prison population starting in the 1980s. In particular, we focus on the role of reactionary forces in setting the tone for mass incarceration through "law-and-order" policies. We examine as well the 1970s economic crisis and how it discredited liberal policies, leading to liberal and conservative convergence on the question of mass incarceration.

We also review the "war on drugs" within this framework.

Finally, we seek to place "crime" in its appropriate context. We examine what is subjectively defined as crime and then look more deeply into the root causes behind actions labeled as "criminal."

With so much attention on the issue, and the wide range of solutions being put forward, we look at solutions for dealing with mass incarceration. More importantly, we offer solutions of our own, and detail the root causes. Finally, we have included a set of biographies of U.S. political prisoners. The vast majority of those who could be qualified as political prisoners in today's U.S. prisons were participants in the mass struggles of the oppressed in the 1960s and early 1970s. Their imprisonment is not only unjust but in fact represents a key link in the chain of mass incarceration. Chapters four and five detail the roots in the "law-and-order" counter-revolutionary rhetoric used by politicians that targeted, slandered, imprisoned and killed numerous individuals and organizations that took a stand against the U.S. capitalist state. The political prisoners cataloged here represent a sample, not an exhaustive list, of those caught up in this dragnet.

Smashing mass incarceration means struggling on behalf of the freedom of these political prisoners, whose sacrifices continue to inspire today. We include this information as a contribution to the fight to free all political prisoners, and raise consciousness around the historical predecessors to radical movements in America today.

As a whole, the book seeks to be not simply analytical but an agent for change. In identifying the key role of capitalist dynamics, we mean no implication that the future of society is preordained. The facts and analysis contained herein are no more than a roadmap to help us understand and plan for overcoming mass incarceration and the modern capitalist system from whence it was born. ☐

Mass Incarceration Today

An overview of mass incarceration

WITH over 7 million people in prison, on parole and on probation in the United States, this country is by far the world leader in incarceration. This shockingly high number is even more remarkable when one considers how quickly it came about. Starting in the 1970s, the U.S. prison population started to trend significantly upwards, before exploding in the 1980s. The numbers provided in this chapter reveal the extent to which the logic of mass incarceration pervades our society. Mass incarceration is a particular scourge on Black communities, functioning as a key instrument of national oppression—that is, the special oppression of Black people as a whole—in the modern era. In fact, if we separate out U.S. prison statistics by gender and race, there is little doubt that the Black man in America is the most hunted, persecuted and incarcerated person in the world.

Examining some worldwide statistics also gives a sense of the massive size of the U.S. prison population. In terms of overall incarceration rates, the United States ranks first, far ahead of all others. China, with a population over four times that of the United States, has about 640,000 fewer prisoners. The number of Black and Latino men alone in state and federal prisons is over 800,000 persons larger than the entire prison population of Russia, the country with the third largest prison system.

While the U.S. position as the world's leading jailer is largely due to the sky-high rates of incarceration among Black and Latino men, as we will see, the system of mass incarceration is not simply a "race issue." The burdens of the criminal justice system fall disproportionately on Blacks, Latinos and Native Americans from the most oppressed communities, but whites with few educational and economic opportunities are likewise incarcerated at very high rates. In fact, if one took just the incarceration rate of white men in the United States, it would still be among the highest in the world.[1]

This is not to say that the prison system is purely a class issue either—even when controlling for class background, there is clearly racial discrimination in conviction and sentencing rates, and the repressive forces of the state reserve their most severe violence for poor communities of color. But the central argument stands: the criminal justice system has a clear class function, funneling poor people of all backgrounds into the mass incarceration complex. Those sections of the population that the capitalist class considers most "superfluous" from the point of view of the labor market receive the worst education, are thus the least skilled, are concentrated in economically devastated "hoods" across the country, and find themselves in nearly daily interaction with the forces of the state. Urban Black and Latino populations have been the prototypical subjects of this mass incarceration system, but the model can be, and to some extent already has been, gradually extended to other sectors.

The criminal justice system has a clear class function, funneling poor people of all backgrounds into the mass incarceration complex.

The country's prison and jail population was 322,945 in 1960 and 338,029 in 1970.[2] Considering the country's overall population growth—from 179.3 million in 1960 to 203.2 million in 1970—the rate of incarceration was essentially unchanged for decades until the 1980s. But from 1985 to 1995, the prison population increased by 622,458, as many of the most important laws regarding mass incarceration were put in place. During those 10 years, the number of people added to prison rolls was nearly twice the number added in the previous 60 years combined.[3] In the same time period, the total number of those in jail at all levels, as well as on probation and parole, rose from just under three million in 1985, to just over five million in 1995.[4] The U.S. prison population never decreased between 1972 and 2010, and currently 7.1 million people fall under the aegis of some section of the so-called criminal justice system.[5] Based on the current statistics, a person living in the United States now is five times more likely to end up in prison than one living in 1925, 1950 or 1975.

As we will later discuss in depth, the transformations in the rates of incarceration cannot be attributed to higher crime rates. Nor can they be attributed to tougher sentencing guidelines, a broader "culture" of law-and-order, right-wing politicians or new policing strategies. These all touch on critical parts of the mass incarceration boom, but often mistake the symptoms for the deeper illness. The phenomenon of mass incarceration is best linked to a phase of high-tech and neoliberal capitalism, in which the economy has been increasingly polarized, large sections of the population have been rendered superfluous to the normal productive process, through technology and "outsourcing," and the government has decisively retreated from its obligations to the poor. The ruling class has utilized the prison system to manage these fundamental transformations, marking a new mass phase in the history of U.S. incarceration. Politically, the capitalist class has carried out this shift in alliance with middle-class sectors by convincing the latter that their security and safety require the strict policing of poor and oppressed communities, including the permanent removal from society of its "dangerous" elements.

THE VICTIMS OF THE PRISON SYSTEM

Incarceration rates by race and gender

The mass incarceration phenomenon has not been distributed evenly across the population, disproportionately targeting men from oppressed communities.[6] Among men in state and federal prison, 39 percent are Black, 31 percent are white, and 23 percent are Latino. A more meaningful way to view these statistics is in proportion to the national population. For every 100,000 Black men, 4,347 are in prison or jail, versus 1,775 for Latino men and 678 for white men. In other words, Black men are nearly six times and Latino males nearly three times more likely to be in prison or jail than white men.[7]

Among women, we see a similar phenomenon. Black women are roughly three times more likely, and Latina women twice as likely, to be in prison than white women. This gap has narrowed considerably in recent years; in 2000, Black women were six times more likely to be incarcerated than white women. In the past decade, however, the rate of incarceration for white women has increased 38 percent, while for Black women it has fallen 35 percent. Latina women have seen an increase of 28 percent. While white women continue to have the lowest overall rate of incarceration by far, it is worth noting that they are in proportionate terms the fastest growing segment of the prison population.[8]

While we will discuss the "war on drugs" in greater depth later, we can note here the enormous impact this false "war" has had on mass incarceration. In 1970, there were 322,300 drug-related arrests, and in 2000 there were 1,375,600. This has hit Black communities particularly hard; during just the 1980s, Black Americans went from 27 percent of drug "criminals" to 46 percent. Drug crimes are punished unevenly by race, with 71 percent of Blacks convicted of drug crimes ending up in prison compared to 63 percent among whites.

These discriminatory patterns persist despite the repeated evidence that Black people do not use drugs at disproportionate rates compared to whites. A National Institute of Health study from the mid-1990s found that out of those they surveyed, 17 percent of whites of the ages 18 to 25 admitted using illicit drugs in the previous month, compared to 16 percent of their Black counterparts. The numbers were reversed with the next oldest age group, with 9 percent of 26- to 34-year-old whites using drugs compared with 11 percent of Blacks of the same age. A Drug Policy Alliance estimates that Blacks are currently 14 percent of "regular drug users," but make up a staggering 37 percent of drug-offense arrests.[9]

The marginalized, homeless and mentally ill

Bureau of Justice statistics reveal that 56 percent of state prisoners, 45 percent of federal prisoners and 64 percent of local jail inmates have a recent history of mental health problems, or related symptoms. One source explains:

> Prisoners have rates of mental illness—including such serious disorders as schizophrenia, bipolar disorder and major depression—that are two to four times higher than members of the general public. Studies and clinical experience consistently indicate that 8 to 19 percent of prisoners have psychiatric disorders that result in significant functional disabilities, and another 15 to 20 percent will require some form of psychiatric intervention during their incarceration.[10]

The report goes on to relate that 23 percent of state inmates and 30 percent of those locked in local jails reported symptoms of major depression. Additionally, 74 percent of state inmates and 76 percent of local jail inmates with mental health issues met the criteria for substance abuse. If all that was not bad enough, state inmates with mental health issues were twice as likely to be homeless before their arrest, and jail inmates with reported mental health issues were three times as likely to have been sexually abused.[11] In testimony before Congress in 2000, Ohio Gov. Ted Strickland estimated that 25-40 percent of all mentally ill persons would in some way become ensnared in the criminal justice system.[12] Arizona's Department of Juvenile Corrections estimates that 25-35 percent of the youth under their supervision suffer from mental illness, and up to 50 percent are taking psychotropic medication of some kind.[13]

> *Arizona's Department of Juvenile Corrections estimates that 25-35 percent of the youth under their supervision suffer from mental illness.*

Alienated youth and the 'school-to-prison pipeline'

We also see a clear relationship between the level of educational attainment and the likelihood of imprisonment. A 1999 study found that amongst African American men between the ages of 30 and 34 who did not complete high school, 52 percent had criminal records as compared to 22 percent for all Black men. Among white men who had dropped out of high school, 13 percent had criminal records, compared to 3 percent of those who graduated.[14]

Mass incarceration rears its ugly head early in the lives of many of those in the most oppressed communities. Draconian discipline policies and insufficient social services create a range of pressures that push many youth out of the school system and into juvenile institutions where the line between the educational system and criminal justice system is often blurred. Some activists and youth advocates have referred to this process as the "school-to-prison pipeline." More or less mirroring the rise of mass incarceration policies in general, the approach towards "problem" children has grown increasingly more punitive, as more and more localities adopt "zero-tolerance" policies that place heavy emphasis on suspension and expulsion. Between 1974 and 2001,

PHOTO: BILL HACKWELL

Schools are increasingly patrolled by police, and students are often arrrested for even minor infractions.

the number of suspensions has increased from 1.7 million to 3.1 million. Not surprisingly, 34 percent of those suspended were Black students, although they make up only 17 percent of the school population.

Further, urban areas around the country have seen drastic increases in the use of police forces to maintain "discipline" on school grounds. Not only have schools become increasingly subject to police control, arrests are often conducted for the most trivial of reasons. In Houston, Texas, for example, 17 percent of school arrests were for "disruption" of classes or on the bus.[15] This is more the norm than an outlier. As one report puts it:

> Zero-tolerance policies impose severe discipline on students without regard to individual circumstances. Under these policies, children have been expelled for giving Midol to a classmate, bringing household goods (including a kitchen knife) to school to donate to Goodwill, and bringing scissors to class for an art project... Children as young as five years old are being led out of classrooms in handcuffs for acting out or throwing temper

tantrums. Students have been arrested for throwing an eraser at a teacher, breaking a pencil, and having rap lyrics in a locker.[16]

These sorts of policies have found support on the federal as well as local level. In 2004, $60 million were provided to school districts to hire more cops to patrol the hallways, and $19 million was awarded to help school districts install "safety-oriented" technology.[17] The country's highest legal authority, the Supreme Court, encouraged this turn in the 1980s with a series of rulings that deprived students of due-process protections afforded to others.

> '*Students have been arrested for throwing an eraser at a teacher, breaking a pencil, and having rap lyrics in a locker.*'

Even when zero-tolerance policies do not lead directly to incarceration, they create a climate that portrays "problem" children as criminals, who are then subjected to all sorts of sanctions (often administered by untrained officials). Suspended students, or those in juvenile justice and other out-of-school "alternatives," often face an even steeper drop-off in their access to educational resources. Children with learning disabilities are represented in juvenile correctional facilities at four times their share of the population.

The narrative is clear: An alienated child, or one who has a tough time learning, acts out; his overworked teacher calls on a school resource officer to remove the child; the child is taken to the "office" (sometimes in handcuffs); he is suspended for one week. Behind in his work, the child's grades suffer more, and he acts out more. After a school fight or subsequent disruption, our student is suspended again, this time for two weeks, and then placed in an alternative school. Fed-up with the situation there, overworked teachers, educational resources that do not relate to his daily life and so on, the student drops out.

A few months later while hanging out with some of his friends who decided to play hooky, the former student is arrested for truancy, petty larceny, vandalism or small-time drug possession. Finally, an unsympathetic judge sentences him to a short stint in the county jail. Now with a criminal record, the former student has even less chance of attaining a job, and resorts to low-level crimes to put some money in his pocket, which inevitably return him to jail. Before long, he is a "repeat offender" subject to mandatory sentencing laws. And "voíla"—the school-to-prison-pipeline.

PRISON PRIVATIZATION

In January 2012, Corrections Corporation of America sent letters to 48 states offering to buy state-run prisons. The offer came with stipulations. The state would have to pay the corporation to operate the prisons for 20 years, and they had to guarantee the prison would remain 90 percent full. The prisons had to have at least 1,000 beds.[18]

> *The mass incarceration boom, while not caused principally by the whims of private contractors, has become deeply intertwined with the 'Prison-Industrial Complex.'*

Developers of a youth prison in Pennsylvania avoided all the legal niceties and went straight to the source, bribing two judges to make sure their prisons stayed full with supposedly criminal children. In this "Kids for Cash" scandal, many were first-time offenders, sent away from their communities and schools for the pettiest of offenses, while the judges raked in millions. One 13-year-old was sent to prison for mocking a school administrator on a social networking site. The convicted judges were sentenced to 15 to 25 years, but the owner of the detention center and financier of the operation received only 18 months in the "cushiest" federal prison in the country.[19]

So much for "reducing crime"—clearly, there are powerful vested interests in and out of government who intend to keep the prisons full. The mass incarceration boom, while not caused principally by the whims of private contractors, has become deeply intertwined with the "Prison-Industrial Complex." A combination of cash-strapped state governments, influenced by powerful corporate lobbies and free-market fundamentalism, gave a huge boost to prison privatization particularly since 1999. In 2010, the number of prisoners held in private facilities has increased to 18 percent of the total prison population, an 80 percent jump from 1999. This period saw a significant rise in the use of prisoners as cheap labor for large corporations, and the contracting out of in-prison services. This has created a whole new web of capital-accumulating interests dependent on a steady stream of incarcerated persons, from phone companies to food contractors. While America's earliest prisons were often private, by 1800 warehousing criminals became solely a responsibility of the state. With the massive spike in incarceration that took place beginning in the 1980s, private prisons reemerged to seize the opportunity for profit. Currently, 30 states have some sort of private imprisonment, and seven house over one-fourth of their prisoners in facilities controlled by private interests. The two largest private prison companies—CCA and GEO Group—had 2010 revenues of $2.9 billion.[20] New Mexico has the highest population of privatized prisoners at 44 percent of those behind bars. From 1994 to 2003, New Mexico was governed by Libertarian Gary Johnson, who proclaimed his opposition to the "war on drugs" but avidly sought the privatization of as many state functions as he could manage, including the prison system.

Private prison companies like to present themselves as simple service providers, meeting the demands of the marketplace and saving governments money. In fact, they have been engaged in quite a bit of legislative pump-priming, working aggressively to enshrine mass incarceration practices in law. Between 1999 and 2009, Corrections Corporation of America alone spent $18 million in lobbying costs. On the federal level they lobby almost every department with any sort of authority over any sort of detention, from the Bureau of Indian Affairs to the Administration for Families and Children. CCA makes sure not to neglect state legislators either, employing 170 lobbyists in 32 states. GEO group, which spent just over $2 million on federal lobbying between 1999 and 2009, had 63 lobbyists in 16 states as of 2010.[21] The lobbyists showered Washington, D.C., with cash to help the passage of the Homeland Security appropriations bill in 2011, which increased funding for ICE.[22]

Private prisons are particularly widespread in the Federal Immigration Detention Center system. Forty-nine percent of all those detained by Immigration and Customs Enforcement are locked up in private prisons. This has been a key growth area for private prison corporations. In 1994, ICE held an average of 5,000 prisoners on any given day. In 2001, this number stood at 21,000, and by the end of 2010 it had jumped to 33,000.

A signal example of the profiteering in the immigrant detention system came to light in the investigations of Arizona's racist Senate Bill 1070. In December 2009, the right-wing American Legislative Exchange Council brought together a number of anti-immigrant legislators, lobbyists and representatives from prison corporations including CCA. One attendee, State Sen. Russell Pearce, introduced SB 1070 four months later and quickly received 36 co-sponsors, two-thirds of whom had been at ALEC's drafting meeting. CCA hired a high-powered lobbyist in Arizona the same week. In the next six months, CCA, GEO Group and Management and Training Corporation poured donations into 30 of the bill's co-sponsors.

> *A report from the Arizona Department of Corrections found that state-run minimum-security prisons were only three cents more costly per day per prisoner than private prisons.*

Jan Brewer, whose star rose in right-wing politics based on her support for SB 1070, even had a former private prison lobbyist as her campaign manager and spokesman.[23] Internal CCA documents stated that immigration detention would create "a significant portion of [their] revenues" in the future.[24] GEO Group President Wayne Calabrese stated their interest succinctly: "Those people coming across the border and getting caught are going to have to be detained and that for me, at least I think, there's going to be enhanced opportunities for what we do."[25]

Even the capitalists' logic for privatizing prisons, that it saves taxpayer money, turns out to be largely false. A 2011 report from the Arizona Department of Corrections found that state-run minimum-security prisons were only three cents more costly per day per prisoner than private prisons. In medium-security prisons, state prisons cost 9 percent less.[26] A 2007 audit in New Mexico found that the state was overpaying $34 million in costs related to the construction of private prisons.[27] Two of the most cited academic analyses comparing costs are inconclusive; privatization is no guarantee of cost savings.[28] Moreover, such arguments often blandly compare government and private prisons, while accepting mass incarceration as a given and failing to consider the impact of private lobbies. The real way to relieve the tax burden is to radically change the criminal justice system and end mass incarceration.

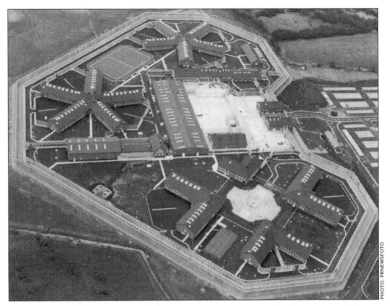

Private prisons, like the one pictured above, seek to turn a profit on mass incarceration.

Cost savings are a totally inadequate way of understanding prison privatization. A better question is how private for-profit facilities treat incarcerated persons. Arizona's private prisons routinely refused to accept those with significant pre-existing health conditions, a sure way to fudge numbers and cut overall costs.[29] In Florida, a state with endemic corruption in state contracting, the two private prisons spent half as much on inmate health care than comparable public facilities.[30]

Even communication with loved ones becomes highway robbery in the U.S. prison system. In a large number of states, telephone service providers charge inmates' families massive fees, and then kick back, on average, 42 percent of the revenue to the states. State prison systems alone rake in $152 million in "commissions" from telephone service providers. Louisiana, for instance, openly stated that their bidding process for the telephone concession would go to those offering the highest percentage of kickbacks.[31]

In states that ban kickbacks, the same telecommunications companies offer significantly lower rates. GTL—one of the largest prison telecommunications contractors—charges families $4.80 for a 15-minute local call in Arkansas, while charging $0.70 in Rhode Island, a non-"commission" state. GTL also charges a $4.75 service for each $25.00 paid into a prepaid phone account, and if the account is not accessed within 90 days the balance will be forfeited into GTL's coffers. Securus, another company, charges a $2.99 bill statement fee, plus a $6.95 processing fee for credit card payments on prepaid accounts. It is absolutely clear that dozens of states deliberately abuse and punish prisoners' families strictly to create new revenue streams for themselves.

PRISONERS AS LOW-WAGE AND NO-WAGE WORKERS

It is not just private prison corporations who reap big profits off inmates. Scores of corporations hire out prisoners to play some role in their operations at very little cost. Prison labor offers a way for companies and states to drive down labor costs and circumvent unionization.

In the federal prison system, all prisoners are required to do some sort of work.[32] Over 20,000 work for Federal Prison Industries (UNICOR), a government-owned corporation that bids for contracts to manufacture a range of items from military clothing, electronic products and components for high-tech weapons systems. UNICOR pays prison workers between $0.23 and $1.15 an hour, far below minimum wage. Prisoners in UNICOR manufacture office furniture, a field where workers outside of prison make on average $13.04 an hour. Compared to prisoners making military uniforms, the average hourly wage for textile workers is $10.95. Not content with old-style industries, UNICOR has even set up a factory to build solar panels.[33] So much for "green jobs" solving the unemployment crisis!

While UNICOR competes for federal government contracts, it cannot sell its goods to the private sector. At the state level, however, there are few such scruples, and state-run prison companies sell their goods in direct competition with private businesses. In the early 1990s, many state legislatures began to pass laws modeled after Texas' "Prison Industries Act." Molded by ALEC, such laws set up a general scheme for prisons to turn their captive populations into a low-wage workforce. While prisoners are supposed to be paid the "prevailing wage," money would be "deducted" from their paychecks to pay for "room-and-board."

These bills also gave private businesses the right to buy goods from prison industries and re-sell them in direct competition with others based on non-prison labor. Florida's 41 prison industries produce tons of processed meats and manufacture furniture and other goods. Its prison-based printing operation has become one of the state's largest. In states like Wisconsin and Virginia, prisoners do a significant amount of the landscaping and upkeep work around state capitols.[34] The City University of New York purchases everything from classroom furniture to exam blue books from the Department of Correctional Services, which is legally stipulated as a "preferred source" for contracts.[35]

On top of this, various large corporations have alternately taken advantage of public-private partnerships to exploit prison labor. As a 2001 BusinessWeek article explains: "Jail-based customer-service centers have fielded 800-line requests for airline reservations. ... [P]risoners have also wrapped software for Microsoft, produced electronic menu boards for McDonald's and stitched clingy lingerie for a manufacturer."[36] Prisoners wrap Starbucks holiday coffees and Nintendo games.

The common rationalization for prison labor is that it lowers the rate of recidivism (re-incarceration). While having a job skill can assist with employment outside the prison walls, the "training" prisoners receive only points them towards a lifetime of poverty wages. Rather than re-enter the workforce at large, in reality ex-prisoners make up another vulnerable set of low-wage, super-exploited workers, sometimes utilized to undermine union labor and prevailing wages in the same industry that employed them inside.

On the whole, prison labor is only a small proportion of the overall workforce and economy. It operates under a variety of restrictions imposed by various business lobbies, denying it free access to the market. One academic study, for example, estimates that "unskilled labor" at most loses a couple hundred dollars due to competition from prison labor.[37] Given the general downward pressure on wages and benefits for almost 30 years, it is clearly in the interest of all workers that such ex-prisoners receive jobs at a living wage and are organized into labor unions. But as with the cost comparisons of public versus private prisons, measuring the impact of prison labor on outside wages or small businesses is an insufficient way of framing the phenomenon. Slave-like prison labor is not just wrong because it lowers wages, but because it is a form of slavery! The argument that prisoners' practically non-existent wages are compensated with "room and board" is nearly identical to the old slaveowners' defense.

The use of prison labor further shows that the capitalist system, not individual failure, is primarily the cause of unemployment in oppressed communities; the very people who are on the outside, both before and after incarceration, are suddenly offered work while incarcerated. ☐

Enter the
torture chambers

TORTUROUS prison conditions are nothing new in the United States, but today's horrendous state of affairs requires special scrutiny. The U.S. government and U.S.-based "human rights" organizations preach constantly about the situation of prisoners in countries targeted for imperialist overthrow, but here prisoners face malnutrition, overcrowding, deeply inadequate health care, physical and psychological torture by guards, torturous long-term solitary confinement and the denial of education services. Prisoners are also often restricted access to various types of reading material, and have their religious and political organizations falsely declared as gangs that are banned from congregating and meeting. A range of onerous restrictions denies regular contact with their loved ones, hurting both the prisoner and the prisoner's family.

OVERCROWDING

Overcrowding is a dominant characteristic of the U.S. prison system. The Federal Bureau of Prisons was operating at 36 percent over capacity at the end of 2010.[1] In 2008, all four federal prisons in New York were at least 50 percent over capacity, with the highest at 61 percent.[2] If this is the situation at the federal level, which has the most resources, it is unsurprising that it is far worse at the state and local level.

In Illinois, 25 of the state's 28 prisons hold more prisoners than they were constructed for.[3] Lincoln Prison, built for 500, has 943 incarcerated persons on any given day.[4] Around the state, prisoners are sleeping on cots in hallways, doubling up in maximum-security cells and showing up in the dead of winter without enough coats or shoes to go around."[5] Despite the existing overcrowding, Illinois Gov.

Pat Quinn has proposed closing some facilities for budgetary reasons, a plan that would require housing thousands of inmates in various gymnasiums.[6]

In Pennsylvania, overcrowding became so severe that the state shipped thousands of prisoners to other states. In Ohio, there are 51,000 inmates, although the stated capacity of its 31 prisons is 38,000. In 2007, half of Kentucky's state facilities were over their stated capacity, while in Alabama the prison system currently runs at 190 percent over its listed capacity.[7] Statistics show that one Alabama prison was operating at 319 percent over capacity in 2009![8] Out of 19 prisons in Massachusetts, 16 were operating above or at 100 percent of their capacity. Built to hold around 8,000 prisoners, the system currently holds over 11,000. In 2011, MCI Concord was at 212 percent of its capacity, while MCI Framingham ATU was, on average, at 281 percent of its capacity.[9] Even Iowa, a state with a relatively small prison population, had a system that was 25 percent over capacity.[10]

> *Statistics show that one Alabama prison was operating at 319 percent over capacity in 2009!*

California state and local prisons have become the exemplars of the problem of overcrowding in the country's mass incarceration system. In 2008, 16,000 prisoners slept on what are known as "ugly beds," bunk beds placed in hallways and gyms and crammed into cells.[11] In May 2011, the overall system was operating at 180 percent of design capacity.[12] The California Institute for Men prison in Chino had twice the number of prisoners that it was designed to hold. Things got so bad that the U.S. Supreme Court ruled that this level of overcrowding violated the Eighth Amendment ban on cruel and unusual punishment. The court ordered the state to rapidly reduce its number of prisoners by 30,000. Tellingly, this meant that the prisons could still operate at 137.5 percent of design capacity.[13] Reception Centers, in which many short-term offenders spend their whole time in California, are even worse in many respects. In Lancaster, Calif., one such center constructed to hold roughly 1,300 prisoners holds close to 5,000 instead.[14]

Although everyone understands the overcrowding epidemic, there has been little political will to change it. Ohio's alleged plans to reduce prison population by 2015 will only marginally improve its overcrowding.[15] A state commission in North Carolina projected in 2011 that the state's prison system would continue to be over capacity at least until 2020, even with measures the state claims will reduce the prison population.[16] North Carolina allows its prisons to legally operate at up to 130 percent of their capacity.[17]

NUTRITION

Despite supposed guidelines, prisoners are denied adequately nutritious food. It is no accident that when prisoners in Virginia went on hunger strike in 2012, their first demand was: "We demand fully cooked food, and access to a better quality of fresh fruit and vegetables. In addition, we demand increased portions on our trays, which allows us to meet our basic nutritional needs as defined by [Virginia Department of Corrections] regulations."

In 2001, it was estimated that the average expenditure on food per person in the United States, on a daily basis was $8.12.[18] But in California, for example, the state spent in 2002 only $2.45 per prisoner per day, having not changed that amount in 14 years despite the rising costs of food. It is not unusual for some states and localities, for example Alabama, to spend less than two dollars. There, the amount of money spent per prisoner per day had not changed since the original government outlay in 1939! Prisoner food expenditures are often one of the key areas targeted for "cost-cutting," and services are frequently contracted out to private companies. Food guidelines vary from prison to prison, with states and the federal government maintaining their own standards or guidelines. The only real oversight comes from prisoners themselves, who file lawsuits regarding food services. This makes it challenging to draw up a detailed national picture on prison nutrition quality. But it is clear that (1) nutrition is treated by authorities as simply a "cost" issue, not a basic human right; and (2) contractors and authorities manipulate the lack of oversight to profiteer off prisoners' nutritional needs.

Virginia and Georgia prisons serve only two meals on weekends. Ohio has similar plans. Georgia denies Friday lunch as well, adjusting its workweek so that inmates now labor four 10-hour days; they are still working the same 40 hours weekly, but with fewer meals.[19] In 2003, Texas ordered prisoner meals to be cut by 200 calories in order to reduce budgetary outlays to prisons.

The Associated Press reported in 2003 that of 34 state legislatures looking to cut budgets, 19 proposed cuts in prison budgets, almost all starting their cuts at "the food tray."[20] One zealous cost-cutter in the Tennessee legislature planned to eliminate Jell-O desserts, but state correctional officials retained it because without it, the prisons would have to actually provide fruit—gasp!—to meet dietary guidelines.[21] The same year, Nevada's governor opposed further cuts to prison food budgets because it had already spent more to feed wild horses under its jurisdiction than human inmates.[22] In Linn County, Oregon, the decision to start serving only cold breakfast was motivated by a mere $40,000 in annual cumulative savings.[23] This is an important lesson to remember when politicians complain about exorbitant prison budgets; few care at all about the conditions for the incarcerated.

> The same year, Nevada's governor opposed further cuts to prison food budgets because it had already spent more to feed wild horses under its jurisdiction than human inmates.

Just as with many other areas of the prison system, and society at large, food services have become increasingly privatized. Absent any meaningful oversight, major food companies like Aramark profiteer off food service to incarcerated persons. In 2010, Aramark attempted to impede an audit from the State of Kentucky of its $12 million contract. The audit showed it had been overpaid and used, against the terms of the contract, $148,000 in free inmate-grown food. In addition, the company kept records that made it impossible to determine if the food it served was nutritionally adequate or safe (which implies that it was neither). The audit found that in some locations, food had been kept too long, and that condiments like margarine were frequently used to make up shortages in required calories, for instance by including it in peanut butter sandwiches.[24] In 2003, state inmates gave the food a 5.8 rating on a scale of 1 to 10, and by 2009, that figure had declined to 3.2.[25] When asked to respond to the state's audit, Gov. Steve Bershear of Kentucky repeated the company line that its food service was a "good investment for the taxpayer."[26]

Kentucky was not alone. In 2008, Florida dropped Aramark as its contractor for prison food service, stating that the state itself could feed more prisoners while saving $7 million by eliminating Aramark's tender.[27] Inmates in Florida's Santa Rosa facility picked up an illness en masse from Aramark-prepared food in 2008, which mirrored a claim the same year when 50 Colorado prisoners were sickened by chili that had been stored at improper temperatures by Aramark.[28] Aramark also seemed unconcerned about violating Georgia rules that mandate that prisoners receive two hot meals a day when, after pressure cookers broke down, they let Clayton County inmates go three months without hot food.[29]

Aramark and others depend on the lax oversight of prison officials as a key element to hide their clear and widespread malfeasance. The Florida Corrections chief-of-staff put it plainly: "[I]n the past we probably didn't manage the contract as closely as we should have." In Tennessee, when numerous prisoners testified to double-digit weight loss, the assigned correctional representative testified that he had neither examined the quantity of food being served, nor did his agency have the manpower to ensure contractor compliance with prison diets.[30]

SOLITARY CONFINEMENT BECOMING THE NORM

The prison system enforces a type of "social death" on those it ensnares. In the literal sense, it removes an individual from society at-large. While this is explained as necessary for the protection of the broader community, it also stigmatizes the prisoner as a permanent outsider. The prisoner is cut off from broader socialization, forcefully disconnected from the cultural, political and social developments of the world. The fact that an ex-prisoner carries a permanent criminal record is a major obstacle preventing the re-integration into the job market. But beyond that, it is common for ex-prisoners who have served long sentences to experience profound and permanent social alienation, somewhat akin to the experiences of veterans who have returned from war. In the movie "Shawshank Redemption," Morgan Freeman's character, Red, put it eloquently: "These walls are funny. First you hate 'em, then you get used to 'em. Enough time passes, you get so you depend on them. That's institutionalized. ... They send you here for life, and that's exactly what they take. The part that counts, anyway."

This social isolation is perhaps most poignant when it comes to losing contact with one's family. Such contact is proven to be an important element in reducing recidivism, but prisons are often placed in rural areas hours away from the cities that they draw from. Even when state buses are provided, they often take so long as to be prohibitive. Telecommunications companies, as discussed before, charge such high rates that it is often economically impractical for many families to talk to incarcerated loved ones on the phone. Bureau of Justice statistics tell us that over half of prisoners with children live more than 100 miles away from their previous location of residence, and 10 percent live over 500 miles away. Visitation is often restricted to a very limited set of hours and days, so even those who can travel to prisons find it hard to schedule visits.[31]

Increasingly, the prison system takes the logic and methods of isolation to their logical conclusion. "Secure Housing Units," "Lockdown," "segregation," "the hole"—whatever you want to call it, the United States is second to none when it comes to imposing solitary confinement on its prisoners. First developed in 1972 at Marion Federal Prison, by 1985 there were about a dozen solitary units in various prisons. The phenomenon then exploded in the 1990s as these "prisons within prisons" and "supermax" facilities proliferated as permanent isolation punishment.[32]

Solitary confinement and extreme isolation have become the norm in many prisons.

Currently 44 states and the Federal Bureau of Prisons use solitary confinement units, nationally holding around 25,000 prisoners in near complete isolation. Bureau of Justice statistics show that from 1995 to 2000 the number of prisoners held in isolation increased 40 percent, as opposed to a 28 percent increase for the prison population at large.[33] Nationally, states average about 1-2 percent of their prisoners in solitary. Colorado has almost 7 percent locked away in isolation, while California's Pelican Bay state prison has 500 inmates who have spent more than 10 years in solitary.[34]

Prisoners held in solitary cells are kept there for 22-24 hours a day, usually with one hour for exercise. Those in solitary often can only shower once a week. They eat inside their cells, which generally have heavy, sometimes sealed, doors and no windows. Those in isolation often have zero access to the already scant education programs, as well as television or radio, and are restricted to a very narrow range of reading material. The already-limited access of friends and family to prisoners is typically even more restrictive or banned outright. Using long-term isolation as a form of punishment is torture.

Studies of the harmful nature of long-term isolation have been in circulation since the 1800s. One source notes that in Germany from 1854 to 1909 at least 37 reports and articles appeared explaining that solitary confinement was the chief cause of inmate psychosis.[35] A large number of reports from around the world have detailed the negative effects of solitary confinement on prisoner health. A 2011 publication issued by the Council of Europe, for instance, deemed more than 14 consecutive days of solitary confinement as "injurious."[36] Previously the Council had pointed out:

> [E]vidence overwhelmingly [indicates] that solitary confinement alone, even in the absence of physical brutality or unhygienic conditions, can produce emotional damage, decline in mental functioning and even the most extreme forms of psychopathology such as depersonalization, hallucinations and delusions.[37]

Summarizing several U.S. studies on the topic, a 2008 report related:

Grassian's (1983) psychiatric evaluation of 14 prisoners held in the solitary confinement block at the Massachusetts Correctional Institution at Walpole reported perceptual changes, affective disturbances, difficulty with thinking, concentration and memory, disturbances of thought content and problems with impulse control. Korn's study (1988) of the women's High Security Unit at Lexington, Kentucky, found that women held there suffered claustrophobia, rage, severe depression, hallucinations, withdrawal, blunting of affect and apathy.[38]

The summary continued, detailing the situation in Pelican Bay State Prison's Secure Housing Unit, which has been the site of multiple prisoner actions and hunger strikes:

Haney's (1993) study of 100 randomly selected prisoners in one of California's supermax prisons, Pelican Bay Security Housing Unit (SHU), reported a very high prevalence of symptoms of psychological trauma with 91 percent of the prisoners sampled suffering from anxiety and nervousness, more than 80 percent suffering from headaches, lethargy and trouble sleeping and 70 percent fearing impending breakdown. More than half of the prisoners suffered from nightmares, dizziness and heart palpitations and other mental-health problems caused by isolation, which included ruminations, irrational anger and confused thought processes (more than 80 percent of prisoners sampled), chronic depression (77 percent), hallucinations (41 percent) and overall deterioration.[39]

One 2007 visitor to the isolation cells in California's youth prisons tells us:

I made a physical inspection of restricted units at Stark, Preston and Chad and generally found that the conditions in these units were deplorable. The cells were dimly lighted, there was graffiti throughout the units, sanitation conditions were below standards of decency in the rooms and in the hallways, and plumbing in the cells worked intermittently or poorly. ... The general living conditions were, in my opinion, oppressive and punitive—certainly not conducive to treatment and rehabilitation.[40]

One Danish study found that prisoners held in an isolation cell were 20 times more likely to later be admitted into a psychiatric hospital.[41] Another study found that the symptoms brought on by isolation can persist for prolonged periods.[42] In particular, long-term isolation can cause difficulty for an individual to interact socially with others, making it tougher to re-integrate themselves into either the broader prison population or society at large upon release from isolation.

Red Onion State Prison in Virginia, for example, keeps over 75 percent of its inmates on 23-hour lock down

A study in Washington State found that those released directly back into their communities from isolation cells were much more likely to end up back in prison.[43]

Mentally ill inmates from the general population are put in segregation at a higher rate. Behavior described as "rule-breaking" casts them into isolation cells as punishment, where access to treatment is even less available and the environment heightens psychological disorders. In 2002, 28 percent of Oregon prisoners in the most "secure" units were acknowledged to be mentally ill. In New York, a study from the mid-2000s found that around one out of every three SHU prisoners had previously been subject to psychiatric hospital care. More than half suffered from depression, 28 percent had either schizophrenia or bi-polar disorder, and the average SHU sentence for mentally ill inmates was six times longer than for those not identified as such.[44] In Arizona, as of 2007, 26 percent of those in the state's two "supermax" prisons are mentally ill. In the state's Maricopa County Jail run by the fascist Joe Arpaio, they do not even consider mental health issues when determining whether to place an inmate in solitary.[45]

The past two decades have seen the rise of "supermax" prisons where almost all prisoners are kept in solitary confinement. Red Onion State Prison in Virginia, for example, keeps over 75 percent of its inmates on 23-hour lock down, in cells that the Washington Post describes as the size of a "doctor's exam room."[46] The average stay in solitary isolation for a Red Onion inmate is 2.7 years.[47] In Texas, once placed in solitary, prisoners have to "earn" their way back into general population; one study found in 2002 that the average length of stay in an isolation cell was 5.2 years.[48] In 2000, all death row inmates in Texas were moved to the Polunsky Unit, where today all 280 prisoners under death sentence are in permanent solitary confinement. The American Friends Service Committee found in 2008 that in California "reception centers," where inmates can be held anywhere from three months to a year, they are confined 23 hours a day with only 30 minutes for lunch and dinner.

> One prisoner with a reggae-related tattoo was even classified as a 'gang of one,' and placed in solitary.

California is also a clear example of how false gang identifications often land prisoners in solitary despite having broken no rules. California prison authorities have the ability to classify any prisoner as a potential threat and lock him down indefinitely.[49] Around half of California SHU prisoners are "validated" gang members—a term which actually means nothing. A 1997 Department of Justice report admitted that 80 percent of validated gang members never had an actual validation process.[50] One can become a validated gang member on the spurious grounds of having contact with an individual who even has the same name as a known gang member. Arizona's validation process is similarly slipshod; the town one comes from can be enough to acquire the mark of "gang member." The only way to be removed from these lists of active gang members is to snitch on members of said "gang." The extreme irony here is that once a person snitches, they then have to be transferred to protective custody, with essentially the same living conditions as their previous solitary cell.[51] Meanwhile, the person they have snitched on may be equally innocent or labeled as a gang member purely on personal grounds.

Clearly this system is constructed to eliminate any bonds of trust between inmates, to isolate those who stand up for themselves, and break up religious and political groups considered potentially subversive. That the Pelican Bay prisoners launched a hunger strike under these conditions, kept in complete isolation from one another, is an amazing feat of heroism that would have been on the front pages of every U.S. newspaper had it taken place in another country.

Massachusetts inmates face a similar situation, where Puerto Rican cultural symbols are considered "gang signs" and have been used to classify a significant portion of all Puerto Rican prisoners as "gang members." One prisoner with a reggae-related tattoo was even classified as a "gang of one," and placed in solitary. In "liberal" Massachusetts, solitary conditions are hellish, and the isolation units have been described in the following manner:

> Every guard on every shift is primed to deal with prisoners there with calculated humiliation. They call people names. Frequent cavity searches, even for prisoners who have not left the block, are used to discourage prisoners from seeking medical help, therapy, or visits. Prisoners who try to fight back, for example by refusing work, have been beaten, tear-gassed, or thrown down the stairs.[52]

Arizona denies supermax prisoners any access to programs that have been proven to reduce recidivism. In California, 69 percent of all suicides in the prison system in 2006 happened amongst inmates in solitary.[53] In New York, 53 percent of those with mental illness who have tried to commit suicide have done so in supermax facilities.[54] Despite the widespread use of such brutal facilities, one 2006 study found that there was absolutely no reduction in inmate violence because of use of isolation cells, and only "mixed support" was found for isolation cells decreasing violence towards prison staff.[55] The only conclusion one can draw from the proliferation of torturous isolation cells in America's prisons is that it is strictly political. Demagogic "law and order" politicians promote cruel internment for reasons that have nothing to do with crime prevention, rehabilitation or even prisoner behavior.

LACK OF HEALTH SERVICES

In the previous chapter, we detailed how the mass incarceration system has locked away an enormous number of mentally ill people. As may be expected, the treatment they receive within the overcrowded prison walls is even worse than the strained, under-funded services offered on the outside. Mentally ill prisoners are routinely subjected to the worst treatment the prison system has to offer. Reviewing this subhuman treatment of the most vulnerable sectors of society offers the clearest signal that the prison system has nothing to do with rehabilitation, reducing recidivism or crime prevention. What possible rehabilitative function could there be to deny basic care to tens of thousands of seriously ill, drug-addicted and often abused individuals, who are placed in situations in which their symptoms are severely aggravated? How could such a scheme reduce crime in the long run?

There are several rough measures of adequate staffing levels for mental health professionals, with the assumption that prisons should provide comparable care to that available to those outside of prison. In 2000, for example, the American Psychiatric Association recommended that each full-time psychiatrist should have no more than 150 patients on psychotropic drugs.[56] A study by the State of Washington recommended "ratios of one psychiatrist for every 200 offenders with outpatient mental health needs." It further called for "one supervising psychologist per institution; one mental health professional for every 75 seriously mentally ill prisoners and one mental health nurse per 100 patients."[57]

While prisons do sometimes have dedicated mental health practitioners, funding for such services is despicably low and crippled by the logic of "tough on crime" politics. Iowa, for example, has only three psychiatrists for the whole system of 2,000 mentally ill inmates. Of the 50 psychologists they employ, the vast majority hold only a bachelor's degree. Arkansas holds 14,000 prisoners but employs only four psychiatrists on the inconceivable grounds that they have a low rate of mentally ill prisoners. A Department of Justice investigation of Wyoming State Penitentiary in 1998 found that in a three-month period, 95 referrals were given, but only six diagnostic exams were performed.[58] Extreme understaffing is common throughout the states given the low salaries and outrageously large caseloads. One corrections official estimated that the average salary for a prison psychiatrist is $20,000 less than what could be obtained elsewhere. A Florida attorney who represents mentally ill prisoners estimated that one-quarter of the mental health positions in those institutions were unfilled.[59] States, municipalities and private contractors then fill holes in staffing with unqualified applicants. For example, Human Rights Watch discovered that in Rhode Island four of the five psychologists in the state system were unlicensed. In one prison in Pennsylvania, only three out of 14 psychologists were licensed, and none had a PhD.[60] In 2001, the mental health system in Alabama prisons was presided over by a psychiatrist who had his license suspended in two states.

> *In one prison in Pennsylvania, only three out of 14 psychologists were licensed, and none had a PhD.*

This understaffing, using burned-out and demoralized health professionals, exacerbates many health-related problems in the prison system. In addition, already adversarial and violent prison guards receive little to no training in dealing with mentally ill inmates, creating a combustible mix in which such inmates are brutalized or criminally neglected. "Malingering" is a common diagnosis given to prisoners who request mental health treatments, with staff often accusing them of faking their conditions in order to obtain better treatment. Frequently, prisoners are not accorded privacy in counseling sessions, further impeding care. Additionally, the lack of staff means medication is often used as the sole treatment for mental illness, with little to no therapy involved. It is nearly impossible for such a regimen to produce positive results. Medication is often used and withdrawn improperly, producing a number of negative symptoms.

Some states are, of course, worse than others. Alabama may be the worst of all. In a state-commissioned report, two researchers summarized their shocking findings in ten points:

1. There is no practical access to needed hospital-level treatment, and the care that is given this designation at Kilby Mental Health Unit does not approximate hospital care.
2. Inmates with serious mental illness report that they frequently must violate rules, hurt themselves or cause property damage to gain the attention of staff. Often even this destructive behavior does not eventuate in treatment; only further disciplinary action and segregation result.
3. The medical records do not reflect adequate treatment planning or interventions and there is simply no way to determine continuity of care.

4. Acutely psychotic inmates are locked-down for long periods of time with little or no treatment. For example, in the case of the Donaldson inmate (125433) who committed suicide on January 11, 2000, the medical records document diagnostic swings from "psychosis" to "never saw evidence of psychosis"; from "clearly paranoid ideation" to "doing fine"; and from pleas for help that go unanswered to a response which is unduly delayed to his completed suicide.
5. Medications are administered in a dangerous and unprofessional manner.
6. Therapeutic programs and counseling are wholly inadequate. Some claims as to providing psychotherapy, both in terms of frequency and what this clinical activity entails, are transparently false.
7. Conditions of confinement in some areas housing inmates experiencing serious mental illness are totally unfit for these very vulnerable inmates.
8. Based on inmate reports and medical record documentation, some mental health staff have demonstrated a general distrust of and contempt for individual inmate patients.
9. The only treatment consistently available is psychotropic medication, but the medication is administered improperly; required monitoring often is not done; and medication is sometimes prescribed without the physician ever seeing the inmate. Medication is not supplemented anywhere we visited by adequate therapy or therapeutic programming. We believe that a prison system which, in practical effect, provides only medication to inmates with mental illness, is grossly inadequate. Treatment for inmates with serious mental illnesses encompasses more than medication.
10. There is little or no evidence of effective training of staff on the rudiments of mental illness and medication.[61]

While court orders have mandated certain reforms, many of the points listed in the above evaluation of Alabama could apply to almost any state. In Virginia's Red Onion supermax prison, Dennis

Webb has spent 14 years in solitary. Diagnosed with both bi-polar disorder and schizophrenia as a child, he was officially listed as having no mental illness for most of his stay. When he did finally see a mental health professional, they spoke only through a door. Another prisoner, Malcolm Springs suffers from borderline personality disorder, depression and bipolar disorder, related to childhood abuse. Springs has tried to kill himself multiple times; he also only gets an occasional through-the-door consultation.[62]

The failure of mental health care in prisons is a nationwide phenomenon, and especially acute given the high rate of individuals in prison suffering from mental illness. While many ruling-class politicians will stand in front of the cameras and explain the need to spend more tax dollars on police and prisons, almost none will go out on a limb to demand spending for prisoner health care. Instead, they focus on developing procedures and regulations that are never implemented but provide political cover when the crisis in prison mental health becomes a media issue.

INACCESSIBLE EDUCATION SERVICES

Bureau of Justice statistics report that 40 percent of state prisoners and 27 percent of federal prisoners have not earned a high-school diploma or GED.[63] While it is clear that insufficient education is not the primary factor causing mass incarceration, nor is it the reason for re-incarceration, several studies show that educational opportunities in prison can significantly reduce recidivism. Dr. Miles Harer's analysis of Federal Bureau of Prisons data found that 30 percent of those who took at least some classes every six months returned to prison compared to 45 percent of those who took none.[64] This trend is broadly confirmed in a series of state-by-state studies.[65] One very relevant fact is that in Dr. Harer's report, 62 percent of the prisoners surveyed had not completed a high-school education.[66]

Despite the clear benefit of having educational opportunities, they are not widely available to prisoners. In 1994, prisoners were stripped of access to federal Pell Grants, striking a major blow to postsecondary education in a wide range of prison systems. Forty-six state prison systems have some educational opportunities, at least on paper, but there are significant differences from one state to the next. In most, very few prisoners have access to them. Eighty-nine percent of prisoners enrolled in a postsecondary program were concentrated in 14 state systems and the Federal Bureau of Prisons.[67] In 2010, California cut $250 million from rehabilitation and education spending. This resulted in 17,000 fewer inmates able to receive vocational and education services, and the layoff of 850 workers who ran GED, vocational and substance abuse programs. California, which has the country's highest recidivism rate at 70 percent, only worsened those statistics by its cutbacks.[68]

The ability for an inmate to improve his or her lot through education is essentially happenstance based on location, and depends on whether they face some sort of administrative restriction. Opportunities are typically limited purely to vocational training—which constitute two-thirds of postsecondary course offerings—unless an inmate pays out of pocket to take a correspondence course. Prison authorities consistently narrow their offerings to that most acceptable to "law and order" ideology, denying study of history and the social sciences, which often lead to growing political consciousness. Instead, they are trained for low-wage jobs.

The majority of prisons place little to no emphasis on any number of proven strategies known to reduce recidivism. The prisons are not meant to rehabilitate, or even reduce crime substantially. They function as human warehouses, enacting a permanent social death on individuals who are of no immediate use to the capitalist system outside the prison walls. They function to remove millions of people who are really just victims of a system, while instructing the rest of the society that these sectors of society are inherently criminal, and their incarceration is necessary for the reduction of crime and violence. In short, the prisons are key instruments for social control. □

Historical Development of the Prison System

The history of
US incarceration

Convict labor has a long history in the development of the United States. English ruling-class figures in fact embraced the early colonial endeavor as a population-dumping exercise. As the spread of capitalist relations caused enormous social disruption, in both the cities and the English countryside, colonial settlement offered an opportunity not only to accrue new riches but also to physically relocate the expanding poverty-stricken and "criminal" sectors of society. Convict labor was a principal feature of the North American colonies, and a large proportion of indentured servants arrived after having been convicted of a crime.

The importation of African slaves expanded through the 1700s and rapidly became the dominant class of unfree labor in the colonial labor market. But indentured servitude and convict labor did not fully disappear until the period following the American Revolution, when the newly independent states in the North gradually abolished slavery and made "free labor"—that is, wage labor—the norm. It is during this period of early capitalist consolidation that the modern prison system formed. From the beginning, the prison institution must be linked to capitalism.

Since the early United States emerged with two distinct but interlinked social systems, capitalism in the North and chattel slavery in the South, it should come as no surprise that the early development of incarceration came with sharp regional distinctions. The most common image that comes to mind of prisons—of specially guarded facilities and prisoners confined to individual cells—originated primarily in the capitalist North. The closer the South moved towards a "free" labor market after the abolition of slavery, the more the form of Southern prisons conformed to what was common in the North.

These emerged as part of an attempt to re-subjugate Black labor. There is, therefore, a significant link between the two region's penal systems: The development of modern prisons took place, in a rough sense, as classes of official bound labor were replaced by "free" wage labor. Capitalist development is deeply entangled with the roots of the mass incarceration system.

NORTHERN PRISONS AND THE AUBURN SYSTEM

Pennsylvania and New York were the vanguard states in Northern prison development. In 1790, the Pennsylvania legislature passed laws at the impetus of the "Philadelphia Society" for the first "modern" prison system. The Quaker state law emphasized the adoption of a cellular system of housing prisoners, which was not particularly new. More innovative was its insistence on the classification of prisoners. Rather than lumping all prisoners together, they were divided into "criminals," debtors and witnesses and segregated by sex. (Women would continue, however, to be kept mostly in distinct parts of the same prisons until 1870.) There was even a provision for solitary cells in Philadelphia's Walnut Street Jail.

Libby Prison housed over 1,000 prisoners in Richmond, Va., 1863. Systemic overcrowding persists today.

PHOTO: LIBRARY OF CONGRESS

While prisoners had often been forced to labor as part of their sentence, the newer model of prison focused on moving that labor inside prison walls, rather than taking place in public. New York followed in 1796 with a similar prison, and several other states quickly followed. Under the pressure of prisoner unrest and other social agitation, however, this mode of imprisonment lost favor in the 1820s and 1830s. It was replaced with the "Auburn system," which dominated in the North and some other states up until just after the Civil War.[1]

The Auburn system was named for Auburn Prison in New York State. Early on, Auburn confined all its inmates in solitary cells without any work requirement. After it became clear that this caused serious mental illness amongst prisoners, the total solitary system was dropped. In its place, inmates were still housed separately but worked together in the prison shop, forced to remain silent. Authorities in the Empire State put a heavy emphasis on operating prison shops profitably, which soon became an attractive feature for other states. The Auburn system also made use of corporal punishment, employing a wide variety of feudal-like techniques that would not be at all out of place in the Tower of London.[2]

The Auburn facility also marked the beginning of an increasing divergence between the treatment of male and female prisoners. Female prisoners at Auburn were crowded into a putrid attic with only one large room, given one meal a day, and mostly kept from working or exercising. Guards routinely whipped female prisoners, until this practice was finally banned after the flogging to death of a pregnant prisoner, Rachel Welch, caused a public outcry.[3] This system of female imprisonment started to decline in New York and other states, which moved to cellular imprisonment by the 1830s as a mild improvement in the living standards for some female prisoners.

In 1867, the dominant Auburn system came under fire after two reformers issued a scathing 600-page report that exposed the lack of prisoner rehabilitation, non-existent or skeletal educational opportunities, unsanitary living conditions and brutal work conditions. This report led to a brief wave of reform, with 12 states adopting a different model based on a prison in Elmira, N.Y., which put greater emphasis on prisoner education. Despite such variations, the roots of the modern U.S. prison system can trace themselves, at least archi-

The 13th Amendment

American history books teach, very straightforwardly, that the 13th Amendment to the U.S. Constitution was the amendment that ended slavery. A close examination, however, reveals that the amendment's first section abolishes slavery only with qualifications:

> Neither slavery nor involuntary servitude, except as a punishment for crime whereof the party shall have been duly convicted, shall exist within the United States, or any place subject to their jurisdiction.

The passage "except as a punishment for crime" has drawn immense attention in recent years from those concerned with mass incarceration. It appears to give legal sanction to free or low wage prison labor in particular. At first glance, it can make the 13th Amendment seem a little hollow, simply a smokescreen for a different sort of racial oppression.

This question of the amendment's true nature, while old, is crucial to how we view the operation of racial oppression in capitalist society, as well as potential solutions to mass incarceration. The 13th Amendment was either a hollow document with the goal of backdoor subversion of the new freedom, or it was an incomplete product of a truly revolutionary process.

The real question though, is the degree to which the 13th Amendment leaves its imprint on mass incarceration today. In the most direct sense, the answer is that there is very little connection between the two. The 13th Amendment is quite clearly not used as justification for the masses of people currently held behind bars. From the point of view of social context however, the 13th Amendment is quite relevant.

The amendment was a product of the struggle of slaves and their allies for emancipation, a necessary stepping stone towards the goal of full equality. As Reconstruction ebbed, the imposition of the Jim Crow system proved to negate that possibility, leaving mass incarceration as one of its legacies today.

tecturally, to the Auburn model, which remains as something of a grandfather to today's prisons.[4]

PRISONS AND THE ABOLITION OF SLAVERY

The American South took a somewhat different course from the North. While early on there were some moves to establish Auburn-style prisons in the South, the pre-Civil War prison system was relatively underdeveloped. With the vast majority of African Americans enslaved, the ability to punish and discipline was left largely to their slaveholders, not the government. Incarcerating a slave, after all, would deprive his master of his labor, and was thus reserved for extraordinary circumstances.

The dramatic end to slavery and the combative politics of the Reconstruction period radically changed this equation. The abolition of slavery in the United States amounted to a thorough social revolution in the South. It overturned the predominant economic system in nearly half the country, threatened the political and economic power of the slave-owning ruling class and laid the basis for the rapid expansion of Northern capitalists' power. On a national level, it called into question the racial definition of citizenship, which had previously been reserved for whites only. Millions of freed slaves were thrust into an uncertain category of supposed freedom.

During the 10 years of Radical Reconstruction, Black communities surged forward, empowered by the Confederacy's defeat, new legal openings and their numerical strength at the ballot box. Those who for centuries had been referred to as a "docile" race showed their combativeness and capacity for self-government, bringing their own political vision to bear on U.S. society.

While slavery's abolition in itself represented a revolution, it opened the door for a variety of monumental struggles over what would replace it. Given that the Southern economy was centered on the plantation labor process, the freedom of the laborer, along with the devastation of the war, seriously disrupted the region's economic center of gravity. Would ex-slaves just filter into the "free labor" market as wage earners? This was the assumption and program of most Northern political leaders, who understood freedom to mean the right to freely contract one's labor. Would the ex-slaveowners be allowed to continue to lead the region? Or would they, now deprived

The 14th and 15th Amendments

The limits of the 13th Amendment became clear fairly quickly, with the abolition of slavery doing very little when it came to inequality between Blacks and whites, either legally or economically. The original Reconstruction plan of President Andrew Johnson pointedly did not include the right to vote, and allowed most former Confederates to regain citizenship rights.

Black Americans and their allies were seeking not only enfranchisement but suppression of vigilante racists, and the redistribution of land to ex-slaves. Across the South in 1865 and 1866, a wave of political conventions swept the Black communities, reflecting the development of "Black politics."

President Johnson was resistant to changes in his plan, determined to return ex-Confederates their previous position. Johnson vetoed the first attempts to pass the Freedman's Bureau Bill and the Civil Rights Act of 1866. However, his intransigence shifted the political center of gravity back to Radical Republicans, who guided through the Civil Rights Act on the second try with the two-thirds' majority necessary to override a presidential veto.

This led directly to the passage of the 14th Amendment, although more watered down than radicals would have liked. It reaffirmed Black citizenship, a step towards granting the demand being raised among Black men for the franchise, but failed to explicitly disenfranchise former Confederates. Congress also passed a new Freedman's Bureau Act that escaped Johnson's veto.

The growing recognition of Black rights by Congress led to an increasing white backlash, and race riots broke out in several Southern cities. It was clear that what had been won on the battlefield could slowly slip away without further action. Congressional elections in the fall of 1866 resulted in victory for Republicans, who gained enough votes to override any presidential veto.

The new Republican Congress enacted legislation granting enfranchisement for Black men, and for suppression of the former Confederate rebels. In 1867, Congress passed the First Reconstruction Act, granting Black men the right to vote at constitutional conventions.

The introduction of several hundred thousand Black men into the electoral process led to the election of biracial, but mostly Black, legislatures in the Southern states, which was the final act needed to pass the 14th Amendment. While not specifically enshrining the right of Black men to vote, it implicitly established that right, and provided Congress with broad discretion to pursue "equal rights" or at least what it interpreted them to be at any given time.

While none of the legislative solutions were a panacea, they were not meaningless. Black agitation, along with that of those whites dedicated to Black equality, drove authorities to consider and then pass laws that at least attempted to overcome the shortcomings of the 13th Amendment, enshrine Black equality in law, protect the right to vote for Black men, and usher in the Reconstruction era, whose promise was true democracy for the former slaves. That these efforts fell short of their goal is of course an important matter, but understanding the context of struggle in which the 13th, 14th and 15th Amendments arose is crucial to how the struggle continues to relate to its past.

of their human property, have their land seized and redistributed? This was the overwhelming yearning of newly freed slaves—for "40 acres and a mule," independent plots of land and the means to till it. This dream to own small plots of land would amount to a meager and tenuous existence in the face of expanding commercial agriculture, but it at least provided independence from direct white control. Would the ex-slaves be given equal political rights, partial rights or no rights? Would the federal government intervene to protect and defend the legal and political gains of the Black communities, or would the South be returned to "home rule"? Who would be armed, and who would be disarmed? Would cotton remain the region's staple cash crop? Would ex-slaves continue to work in the cotton fields as wage workers (but now paying for their food, clothes and shelter)?

This history matters to the present discussion of mass incarceration, because in the immediate aftermath of slavery we observe the first real boom in the prison population. Southern plantation owners, suddenly deprived of their captive labor force, used the legal system to make up the difference. A series of laws, called Black Codes, specified which occupations were open to the now "free" Black population. They declared that those who failed to sign yearly labor contracts could be arrested and hired out to white landowners. In some states, they barred Black land ownership. They created a wide array of laws to entrap Black labor, like traveling without a pass or loitering. Those who could not pay their fine would be arrested, and their fine would be auctioned off to a white employer in return for labor. The sight of young Black men and women on the auction block reappeared, as if it had never gone away.

> *The criminal justice system became a way to funnel common laborers back to the plantations and for white employers to stifle radical voices.*

The outrage against these Black Codes created the stimulus for the 14th and 15th Amendments to the Constitution and the Radical Reconstruction period that followed. The Black Codes were largely nullified in this process and defeated by Black political mobilization. But the strength of Reconstruction varied from place to place based on the level of organization within the Black community, the amount of violence meted out by the Southern ruling class and armed Klan terrorists, the varying commitments of local Republican Party organizations and the shifting loyalties of poor and middling white farmers.

Thus, even over the period of Radical Reconstruction, many areas gradually fell back under the control of the counter-revolution. One immediate sign of these political losses came in the prison statistics. As the forces of white supremacy recaptured the states, they utilized this position to incarcerate growing numbers of Black people. The criminal justice system became a way to funnel common laborers back to the plantations and for white employers to stifle radical voices. It also became a way to incarcerate political "trouble-makers."

The conservative "Presidential Reconstruction" governments quickly passed a range of "Black Codes" in 1865 and 1866 designed to restrict the mobility and economic opportunity of Blacks. Across the South, broadly defined "vagrancy laws" ensnared many, requiring fines and labor. Some states' codes, like Mississippi, required Blacks to show proof of employment each year, and in a holdover from the slave patrols, allowed any white citizen to arrest a Black "lawbreaker."

High-tax barriers were sometimes erected to limit Blacks from owning land, and some states established "apprenticeship" programs that allowed employers access to free labor from Black children. The rise of Radical Reconstruction prevented some of these codes from truly going into effect, but many others, such as the "vagrancy" statutes, continued on, stripped of racial language. This significantly limited the economic and social mobility of freed slaves, while protecting the revived planters and the treasure-seeking Northern entrepreneurs eager for profits in the resuscitation of the Southern economy. The Black Codes, while functioning through the criminal justice system as part of the state, did not exist primarily to put people in prison institutions; on the contrary, they existed to recreate a class of subjugated labor, to maintain Blacks working principally in the plantation and service economy.

THE JIM CROW PERIOD AND CONVICT-LEASE LABOR

Jim Crow segregation did not emerge immediately after the abolition of slavery, instead coming out of the defeat of Radical Reconstruction as the consolidation of the political counter-revolution. It was designed principally to constrict Black labor to semi-feudal agriculture and to prevent the resurgence of Black or interracial political challenges to white supremacy. The prison was not the central institution of Jim Crow rule—the rate of incarceration among Black people then was considerably lower than it is today. Instead of mass incarceration, a broader system of white supremacy—enforced by law, custom and violence—kept the majority of Blacks tied to the land in a serf-like existence or forced to seek the least desirable employment in industry, mining and service-sector work. The capitalist-minded leaders of the "New South," who sought to modernize and industrialize the region, comfortably adapted Jim Crow segregation to the organization of the workplace, and the prison system helped them relieve labor shortages.

Part and parcel of Jim Crow oppression was the convict-lease labor system. Convicted people were "leased" by the government to work without pay for private corporations, allowing both government and the owners to rake in exorbitant profits. Both "progressive" industrializers in the South and its old aristocrats utilized this form of labor, which was almost exclusively Black, from the first years

PHOTO: LIBRARY OF CONGRESS

Convict labor has long been a method to exploit prisoners.
Here, a road gang in Pitt County, N.C.

after emancipation into the 1920s. Convict-lease was not the South's dominant labor system, but did figure prominently in several key industrial sectors. In 1890, the number of convict laborers stood at 27,000: a significant, but not overwhelming figure.[5] But iron and coal in particular, which had been held in a very low state of development during slavery, were heavily dependent on convict-lease labor, as was railroad construction. As scholar Alex Lichtenstein has argued, convict-lease operated as a large-scale state subsidy to these industries, and in coal played a particularly important role, given the shortages of free workers for this dangerous work.

Convict-lease laborers were not human chattel owned outright by individual masters, but in the conditions of work such distinctions were often irrelevant. In fact, it could reasonably be argued that conditions were more brutal than slavery; as some writers have discovered, Mississippi convict laborers rarely lived a long enough life to complete a 10-year sentence.[6] In Georgia, prisoners were ruthlessly whipped and beaten by bosses who reveled in their total authority. Scholar Matthew Mancini relates a practice of dragging the whip through sand between every lash as a common way to increase the pain. One report to the governor of Georgia stated, "I am fully satis-fied that a humane treatment of them is entirely ignored."[7] Govern-ment officials of the time noted that the corporate prison bosses, who had acquired their Black laborers on the cheap, were more willing to beat, work and starve them to death than the slave-owners decades earlier who had invested large sums in their human property. The severe brutality of the system went far beyond economic rationale, however, reflecting the capitalist overseers' deep racist contempt for the Black people under their authority.

Underscoring the particular social context of convict leasing was its transformation into, and replacement by, the chain-gang system. The growing need for roads in the South resulted in prison laborers being shifted out of the private labor sector and into the development of public infrastructure. In short, the government transitioned from slave-catching and slave-selling to using these new-age slaves for its own purposes.

IS THE CURRENT MASS INCARCERATION PHENOMENON THE 'NEW JIM CROW'?

A succinct name or explanation—like Michelle Alexander's "The New Jim Crow" can be hard to resist. The parallels are clear and evocative: They are systems that are discriminatory to their core, disenfranchise millions of Black people, and keep Black America as a whole held to a subordinate status. But the analogy has its limita-tion—as Alexander admits—and the term can also become mislead-ing, obstructing an analysis of the socioeconomic forces that underlie mass incarceration.

An essential feature of the Black Codes and the convict-lease labor system was their ties to the new social and productive relations in the South. The Black Codes played a key role in preserving a form of the plantation labor system, while the leasing system provided an initial labor force for upstart Southern industries. As Radical Recon-struction was defeated by a vicious counter-revolution, the criminal justice system worked alongside mob rule and lynch law to limit Black mobility and opportunity, setting the racial boundaries to a new system of exploitation—not just oppression on the basis of race alone.

The persistence of racist oppression in the U.S. legal system, and society as a whole, is an undeniable fact. But to understand the development of racism, white supremacy and national oppression in the United States requires linking these great evils to the overall political economy of the country. It is accurate but ultimately insufficient to say that racism simply reinvented itself from slavery to Jim Crow to the New Jim Crow. White supremacy and racism are not floating in the air as independent and anonymous forces with the power to restructure society. They operate in tandem with, and ultimately are subservient to, the evolving capitalist economic structure. Thus, slavery was not just racial oppression, but a system based around a particular form of labor super-exploitation. Jim Crow, too, was designed and continuously redesigned to secure and suppress Black labor in the region's planter-dominated agriculture and low-wage industries.

How does this compare to mass incarceration? As modes of social control and national oppression, slavery and Jim Crow were designed around Black people actually laboring. Mass incarceration, by contrast, is a political and state response to the masses of Black people being thrown out of the productive process altogether. Mass incarceration was constructed, notwithstanding the role of prison labor, in a period of high-technology in which the capitalist class decisively sought to minimize labor costs, and launched a concerted effort to eliminate social services. Instead of Northern and Western cities serving as the "promised land" for African Americans migrating from the South, these migrants entered the capitalist economy at the lowest rungs, and repeatedly were the first to suffer from de-skilling and layoffs. Kept out of the labor market, huge numbers of African Americans were trapped in either neglected inner-city "hoods" or the cruelties of the prison system, severely inhibited from agitating for better conditions or a new social system.

There are a few other critical differences between Jim Crow and mass incarceration. Jim Crow was a system that essentially governed all public life for all Black people. While racism penetrates every level of the criminal justice system, mass incarceration affects poor and working-class Black communities much more severely than middle- and upper-class individuals. Jim Crow was based on near complete disenfranchisement of Black people of all social classes, with no pretense of legal and political equality. While mass incarceration does disenfranchise hundreds of thousands, it does not require the wholesale elimination of Black political participation. The mass incarceration period in fact coincides with the election of Black politicians to many of the country's most esteemed offices, including the presidency.

The changed social function of mass incarceration, in comparison to slavery and Jim Crow, is a crucial analytical and strategic issue for people who want to see it dismantled. These various periods are undoubtedly linked by the permanence of racial discrimination and oppression. That a Black man stands at the head of the capitalist government, however, reinforces the changed political conditions of the present struggle and draws our attention ever more sharply to the class realities at the foundation of mass incarceration.

A movement against the prison system, in which the principal subjects are poor and working-class Black and Latino people—along with an increasing number of poor whites—must pose the following questions: What sort of economic system will guarantee jobs and income to the people? What sort of economic system will use technological advancement for the benefit of all of society, instead of a means to throw people out of the productive process? What sort of economic system will devote the resources to eradicate the scourge of drug addiction, to flood the schools with resources instead of cops and metal detectors? What sort of economic system will put poor and working people in power, make them the leaders of society rather than its perpetual victims? Certainly not the capitalist system.

In the following chapters, we attempt to sketch a broad history of how and why mass incarceration developed when it did. Those who are dedicated to uprooting the brutal system of mass incarceration must, of course, look for slogans and concepts to popularize this cause. But likewise, we must strive for a theory of mass incarceration with unimpeachable explanatory power—a clear analysis that shows how we got here, what social processes are driving the phenomenon, how the system can be uprooted and what should replace it. □

Revolution
in the air

IN August 1971, a lawyer for big tobacco in Richmond, Va., sent a memorandum to an acquaintance at the U.S. Chamber of Commerce with the ominous title: "Attack on American Free Enterprise System." His memo expressed alarm that not only were the "Communists, New Leftists and other revolutionaries" involved in said attack, but the anti-capitalist fervor drew from "perfectly respectable elements of society: from the college campus, the pulpit, the media, the intellectual and literary journals, the arts and sciences and from politicians." Their collective efforts were nothing less than a "shotgun attack on the system itself."

The author of the memo was Lewis Powell, who would go on to become a Supreme Court justice several years later. The Powell Memorandum offered not only a diagnosis of the social problem but a comprehensive remedy: for capitalist corporations to launch a counter-attack in all arenas to stop the rising tide of revolution. While it is difficult to measure the impact of the Powell Memorandum itself, the document is an important indication of the mood of the times, including the thinking of the U.S. ruling class. Today the mainstream media portrays the late 1960s and early 1970s through stereotypical cultural and generational clashes, but in reality it was a period of enormous social turmoil that raised the idea of revolution—both for those who hoped for it, and those who feared it.

The mass incarceration phenomenon is rooted in this period as well, as reactionary politicians responded to the social disruptions with conservative "law and order" politics. They lumped mass protest movements with criminality and, in the case of the Black liberation movement, "ghetto" pathology. They created a perception of wild anarchy, in which all the fundamental institutions of society—the government, the "free" market, the military, the police, the family and many others, including white supremacy—were all under threat. Such a portrayal facilitated the militarization of police and created the climate in which varied classes and strata in America accepted the logic of harsh and expanded imprisonment techniques.

THE POSTWAR SOCIAL CONTRACT

In the immediate years after World War II, few ruling-class politicians would have predicted that the country would be convulsed in a dramatic social crisis within a generation. They would have scarcely believed the Powell Memorandum's horror story—of the capitalist system widely questioned and under assault from every generation. During those years, capitalism in the developed Western countries rested on an implicit compact between classes that promised a steadily rising standard of living. As these economies grew, the benefits of growth were to be experienced by all, making the Great Depression and hardships of war appear ever-more distant memories.

While these developed capitalist societies remained sharply class-divided, the capitalists employed a multitude of mechanisms to curb the excesses and sharp polarization that characterized earlier periods. The rate of taxation on the rich remained relatively high by today's terms. Corporate giants finally granted labor unions' place at the table, which through collective bargaining agreements steadily improved the wages and benefits of their members. This in turn lifted the average wages and conditions of non-union workers. In the United States, the government backed low-interest loans for millions of working-class families to become homeowners. The development of the public university system and initiatives such as the GI Bill gave millions more access to a college education and the white-collar jobs that came with them. On a world scale, the supremacy of the U.S. dollar as the means of exchange and payment stimulated the consumer economy. Large sections of the population could enjoy things—automobiles, homes, family vacations, televisions and other household items—that would have been out of reach for their parents, lending a material basis to the idea that the United States promised social mobility, as a society where "anyone can make it."

The U.S. ruling class pursued this strategy in the context of the global class struggle between capitalism and socialism. The Soviet Union offered a different model, which within a few decades had taken one of Europe's poorest countries to a first-rate power. It guaranteed jobs, housing, free education and health care as universal rights, while making historic strides in science, the status of women and the position of oppressed nationalities. For both domestic purposes and most critically on the international stage, U.S. policymakers understood the necessity of advertising the material rewards and opportunities of capitalism. Through the 1950s, they harshly repressed those radicals who, refusing to toe the line, continued their advocacy for socialism and class struggle. Meanwhile, the ruling classes of Europe quickly adopted aspects of the socialist system—such as universal health care and an expansive welfare state—so as to forestall revolutionary agitation.

The Black freedom struggle, which went through successive stages of radicalization, inspired other oppressed sectors into action...

In the United States, there existed several glaring contradictions to their celebration of capitalism, and chief among them was the grinding oppression and blatant double standard facing Black Americans. Discriminated against in every field, segregated, subjected to racist police and mob violence and politically disenfranchised, Black people were essentially left outside of this new social contract. This contradiction erupted in the mid-1950s, and for the next 10 years the civil rights movement captivated the country with its heroic efforts to knock down segregation and win the constitutional liberties and equal protections long denied to Black people. While some commentators and historians incorrectly describe this movement as an "integration struggle," in reality "freedom" was the word on everyone's lips and the movement's animating idea.

The Black freedom struggle, which went through successive stages of radicalization, inspired other oppressed sectors into action, including Chicanos, Puerto Ricans, Asian Americans, Native Americans, women, and gays and lesbians. Combined with the faltering and ultimate defeat of the U.S. war machine in Vietnam, and the spreading anti-colonial movements worldwide, it appeared that the U.S. ruling class was under assault from all sides. And losing.

URBAN UNREST AND THE BLACK LIBERATION MOVEMENT

In the original draft of his speech to the 1963 March on Washington, Student Non-violent Coordinating Committee Chairman John Lewis expressed the more vexing questions raised in the course of the monumental struggle against Jim Crow segregation:

> We march today for jobs and freedom, but we have nothing to be proud of, for hundreds and thousands of our brothers are not here. They have no money for their transportation, for they are receiving starvation wages or no wages at all.... What is there in this bill to ensure the equality of a maid who earns $5 a week in a home whose income is $100,000 a year?[1]

Lewis' key point was the seemingly permanent and racist character of inequality in the United States. Even as the apartheid walls of Jim Crow came tumbling down, the majority of Blacks still lived a precarious existence in either urban slums or impoverished rural areas. This was as true in the supposedly "free" North as the South. Black people experienced extreme and disproportionate poverty, unemployment, denial of social services, red-lined neighborhoods (which they were prohibited to move into), police harassment and racist work environments. Even where legal and formal equality was already the norm, the networks of capitalist power had already entrenched bigotry in a much more profound way.

In this context, the civil rights movement began to turn decisively to challenge social and economic inequality, issues that had long been present but largely submerged under the fight for equality under the law. Inspired by the anti-colonial movements worldwide, many arrived at the conclusion that Black communities needed not just equal rights as citizens but liberation from white America. In this expanding Black liberation movement, a range of organizations, reflecting disparate class and political backgrounds, stepped forward to offer their program for how real equality could be achieved. The Black liberation movement shifted the regional basis of protest activity away from the South to the cities and suburbs of the North and West, which had long considered themselves more enlightened than their Southern counterparts.

The problems of the urban "ghettos"—slum conditions, unemployment, job discrimination, oppressive policing and an unresponsive political system—could also be found in the South in one form or another. But because African Americans in the North already possessed many formal legal rights, including the vote, the struggle there took a radically different form. Unlike in the South, where "whites only" was open law, in the North this racist principle was reinforced in the "free" market: employers who would not hire, real estate developers who would not sell, bureaucracies that would not deliver, politicians that would not respond, courts that would not prosecute abusive police. How do you fight white supremacy in a political system that publicly disavows it? How do you fight poverty in a system that says "equal opportunity" is already the rule?

These were the hotly debated questions of the movement. "Black Power" emerged as a slogan and concept in the mid-1960s as an answer. The notion of "Black Power"—Black political, economic and cultural control over Black communities—could appeal to individuals who advocated a range of political philosophies and strategies. It had liberal and social-democratic variants, as Black representatives utilized the reorganization of voting districts spurred by the Voting Rights Act to take hold of government offices. It took more separatist expressions, as some groups sought to construct an independent Black political state in the South. Others employed the slogan primarily to build independent Black cultural and community institutions, which would help foster a united Black or pan-African identity. It could also take on varied meanings for Black socialists. The League of Revolutionary Black Workers demanded power at the workplace and over the means of production. The Black Panther Party emphasized organized Black self-defense and the building of a revolutionary multinational united front that would ultimately overthrow capitalism.

All these political trends were responding, in one form or another, to the series of explosive urban uprisings that took place in the North, Midwest and West Coast in the late 1960s. African Americans nationwide were deeply connected to and inspired by the struggles of the South. But given the critical differences from one region to the

Racism and urban poverty gave rise to rebellions across the country in the late 1960s.

other, the non-violent tactics and strategies that dominated at one stage of the struggle could not simply be imported and repeated. In 1964, after the NYPD killed a Black teenager in Harlem, police charged at a protest of thousands, which set off five days of unrest in Harlem and across the city. Over 6,000 police were needed to quell the "disturbances." In August 1965, a traffic stop in the Watts area of Los Angeles turned into a major confrontation between neighborhood residents and police. Supposedly routine traffic stops had long served as a cover for harassment, and on that night local residents attempted to intervene to prevent the arrest of a Black motorist accused of drunken driving. Police were able to arrest the driver, along with his brother and mother, leaving the angry crowd simmering. That night, the anger boiled over into five days of "rioting." At its peak, over 13,000 National Guardsmen were sent to Watts to restore order. Over 200 buildings were damaged in Watts, mostly white-owned businesses where usurious prices and discrimination had bred resentment. The governor's report on the uprising stated: "We note with interest that no residences were deliberately burned, that damage to schools, libraries, churches and public buildings was minimal."[2]

While the "rioters" in Watts and Harlem were described as "animals" and unruly hooligans, their actions clearly had a political character. This was understood as much by the government authorities as by Black political activists. In 1967, President Johnson convened the National Advisory Commission on Civil Disorders, or Kerner Commission, to study the rash of "riots" in the country.

Although the report offered a false pathologized view of "ghetto" inhabitants, it diagnosed such problems as a result of social conditions and principally "white racism." The report highlighted "pervasive discrimination and segregation," which resulted in "the exclusion of great numbers of Negroes from the benefits of economic progress."[3] Further, there was a "crisis of deteriorating facilities and services and unmet human needs," in the "ghettos where segregation and poverty converge on the young to destroy opportunity."[4] In a poll taken by the Urban League shortly after the 1967 Detroit rebellion, at least 44 percent of respondents stated that police brutality, overcrowded living conditions, poor housing, lack of jobs and poverty had "a great deal to do" with the cause of the uprising.[5] A poll conducted in Watts found that 64 percent of those living in the curfew zone felt that "discrimination," and "deprivation" were key causes of the uprisings, while another poll found 58 percent of surveyed Watts residents citing "economic problems" as the central cause.[6]

It is worth noting that the uprisings that swept the nation during the 1960s found significant, if not majority, support amongst African Americans living in affected areas. In the Newark riot of 1967, 45 percent of Black males from the ages of 15 to 35 identified themselves as rioters.[7] In Detroit, 30 percent of Blacks surveyed were "highly sympathetic" to the riots, while in Oakland 50 percent felt riots would be "helpful."[8]

The uprisings or "riots" during the 1960s and early 1970s numbered in the hundreds. The Kerner Commission reported 164 "disturbances" in 1967 alone, eight of which were "major," 33 of which were "serious."[9] Another study states that from 1964 to 1968 there were 329 riots "of significance."[10] The pattern of Black uprising was thus woven into the social experience of the period. It had a decisive impact on the mood and organizational forms within the Black communities, and within white communities whose perceptions of the events were heavily filtered through ruling-class media and politicians.

From the mid-1960s into the early 1970s, such politicians tended to respond with a mixture of carrot and sticks—immediate and violent repression combined with expanded social services and programs. The Johnson administration expanded the "war on poverty," a program initially conceived to address poverty in mostly white Appalachian regions, into urban centers as a way to address the systemic problems identified by the Kerner Commission. Liberal commentators tended to portray the urban unrest as a consequence of longstanding government negligence; new social programs, improved services and job training, they proclaimed, would deliver the equal opportunity that the country promised. As we will see in the following chapters, this view was challenged sharply by the ascendant right wing, and as the economic ground shifted, liberals themselves made a decisive retreat away from social programs.

VIETNAM, STUDENTS AND RANK-AND-FILE RESISTANCE

The June 1971 issue of the Armed Forces Journal carried an article with the eye-catching title "Collapse of the Armed Forces." Written by Col. Robert Heinl, the article described significant "decay" in the ranks of the armed forces, the seriousness of which was underscored by his first sentence: "The morale, discipline and battleworthiness of the U.S. Armed Forces are, with a few salient exceptions, lower and worse than at anytime in this century and possibly in the history of the United States."[11] The Marine Corps Gazette echoed this message, with a top training officer declaring that the service experienced "more problems today than ever before."[12]

Soldiers were refusing to fight. In 1969, an entire company in Vietnam simply sat down on the battlefield, and another refused to carry out a mission while being filmed by a CBS television crew.[13] During the five-year period when the U.S. Army was most heavily committed in Vietnam, the desertion rate increased 400 percent. The 1971 rate was three times higher than that of the Korean War.[14] In the Air Force, similar trends can be observed where between 1968 and 1971 desertion rates jumped 300 percent. In 1972, in just one month, the Navy had three mutinies.[15] In 1970, the U.S. military admitted fraggings—killings of unpopular officers by men under their command—had doubled in just a year. By 1971, they were running at the rate of one per week in one division.[16] The death of officers even drew cheers during "troop movies."[17]

Even with conscription, the military found it difficult to maintain appropriate manpower levels. Open draft resistance was widespread with tens of thousands simply refusing to show for induction. In the six months between the end of 1969 and March 1970, over 50 percent of those called did not show.[18] In fiscal year 1972, more people filed for conscientious objector status than were called up in the draft.[19] Other soldiers simply checked out, using drugs to escape. In 1970 alone, the Navy discharged 5,000 sailors for addiction. That same year, the Army conducted almost 18,000 investigations into drug use.[20] In one battalion in Germany, over 50 percent of soldiers stated they used marijuana and many smoked on duty.[21]

> *Tens of thousands of GIs became an active part of the anti-war movement, and played a significant part in building anti-war consciousness amongst the broader population.*

Much of the turmoil inside the Vietnam-era military was politically motivated. Tens of thousands of GIs became an active part of the anti-war movement, and played a significant part in building anti-war consciousness amongst the broader population. The Vietnam Veterans Against the War "Winter Soldier" hearings in the early 1970s were the first time in the United States that war crimes by U.S. troops were widely aired. It followed in the footsteps of the 1967 Russell-Sartre Tribunal, which exposed U.S. war crimes in Indochina to the world.

The conflicts within the military had riven society more broadly. Desertions even hit the establishment, as 200 State Department employees resigned after Nixon's invasion of Cambodia. Hundreds of campuses were shut down with strikes over the Cambodian invasion and killings by the National Guard police at Kent and Jackson State Universities. Massive unrest spread across the nation's colleges as state repression at home and abroad was assailed by protesting students.[22] Many of these protests turned militant, and in the ivory tower the ROTC were persona non grata. Students at Kent State torched the ROTC building after the invasion of Cambodia, and military-affiliated research operations on campuses were often vandalized or destroyed. Planned May Day 1971 protests to "shut down the government" so alarmed Nixon administration officials that Washington, D.C., was put into a fascist-style lockdown. Tens of thousands of soldiers and police were deployed to secure monuments and open space. Authorities roamed the streets arresting people at will in large-scale sweeps, and often using tear gas. Over the three days of protests, a record 12,000 demonstrators were arrested.

SUMMARY

While a full discussion of the social movements of the 1960s and early 1970s is beyond the scope of this book, the examples above are representative of the climate in the country at the time. Much more can be said about these movements, but the fundamental point is that their collective size and energy stoked the fires of revolution in the hearts of significant sectors of the population, and a desire for "progressive" reform even more broadly. They also set fire to the slower-burning coals of counter-revolution in which "law and order" entrenched itself as the underlying principle of U.S. policing and imprisonment. To that subject, we now turn. ☐

Nixon promises order

The law-and-order response

DEMAGOGIC "law and order" politicians stepped forward in the 1960s to rally the broader social forces that felt challenged by the Black, feminist and anti-war movements. In his 1968 election, Richard Nixon portrayed the Republicans as the party of order. He promised to reverse the "anarchy" that the Democratic Party had facilitated, to tame the lawless elements, while bringing rising incomes, and an "honorable" disengagement from the Vietnam War. He aimed to construct a new political constituency from those he called the "Silent Majority"—the law-abiding, patriotic and hard-working Americans whose interests had been overshadowed by rioters, radicals, hippies and traitors. The racist meaning of this slogan was clear enough and his aim was to slice white suburbanites, blue-collar workers and southerners away from the Democratic Party coalition.

While Nixon's economic policies remained in the same liberal Keynesian framework as his Democratic competitors, his law-and-order platform spoke to the emergent New Right, which embraced a crackdown on dissent. It was also a point of unity with liberal Republican Nelson Rockefeller, as well as white ethnic patronage networks and Democratic political machines across the country feeling the pressure of African American political challenges.

In addition to the political unrest, there was a simultaneous uptick in crime in the late 1960s and early 1970s across a variety of categories. Nixon and the Republicans connected this crime with the social turmoil of the period, using the breakdown of "law and order" to explain rapes, muggings and murders alongside uprisings, campus protests and revolutionary activity. Republicans blamed liberals' "excessive tolerance" of "deviant" behavior. Vice President Spiro Agnew explained: "By rationalizing crime and violence and attributing it to lofty causes, they have contributed to it."[1] Time magazine explained the Republican political message: "[T]he permissive attitudes of radic-libs have led to a youth revolution, slackening moral standards, disrespect for order, rocketing rates of crime and dope use."[2] Nixon also aimed to reverse recent civil liberties victories in the court system, which he claimed coddled criminals. In particular, Nixon took aim at the *Miranda, Wade,* and *Gilbert* decisions. *Miranda* stated that evidence obtained through interrogation was legally admissible only if the police had informed the accused of their right to remain silent and to have a lawyer present. Nixon was indignant, ridiculously claiming that only "one in eight" so-called "major" crimes had resulted in conviction as a direct result of *Miranda* and other rulings.[3] The *Wade* and *Gilbert* decisions dealt with the conditions under which evidence obtained from police line-ups could be admitted into court. In 1968, Nixon appeared in front of the Senate to support a crime bill that sought to invalidate *Miranda* and increase police powers. The thrust of Nixon's testimony in front of the Judiciary Committee was to stake a position in favor of order at all costs. He derided a "barbed wire of legalisms," that gave a "green light" to "criminal elements."[4]

This right-wing campaign for law and order was not just one of words. It had real consequences, which included 1) a full-scale crackdown on revolutionary organizations, 2) the rapid expansion and militarization of police forces, 3) dramatic spending increases in corrections and 4) the erosion of the liberal response to urban crime. These factors would ultimately pave the way towards the mass incarceration boom.

COINTELPRO

Having portrayed political radicalism as the incubator of a "lawless" environment, Nixon cracked down hard on the Black liberation movement. Agnew described the Black Panthers as "anarchistic criminals," while the Justice Department branded the BPP as simply "hoodlums."[5] "Law and order" was not simply a rhetorical strategy for political elites to deploy during campaign season. It provided an explanation for the most radical movements to be undermined through subterfuge and extreme violence. These strategies would come to be known collectively as COINTELPRO, after the FBI's Counter-Intelligence Program. In league with local police units, the FBI declared war on political radicals and militant groups from nationally oppressed communities. Most centrally, the government directed its efforts at the Black Panther Party, which FBI Director J. Edgar Hoover deemed the "greatest threat" to America's internal "security." While government repression touched a wide range of organizations and individuals, we outline below only briefly the campaign targeting the Black Panther Party.

> Why did the Panthers threaten the U.S. government so much? It was terrified that they had the ability to put forward leaders to channel the mass defiance of the 1960s, growing especially militant among African American communities, into a potent revolutionary movement. Hoover instructed his agents to: prevent the coalition of black nationalist groups; prevent the rise of a messiah who could unify and electrify the militant black nationalist movement...and prevent the long-range growth of militant black nationalist organizations especially among the youth.[6]

The Panthers' revolutionary socialist perspective further made the organization a permanent enemy of the state, whose program could not be bought off through simple reforms. U.S. Attorney General John Mitchell stated in 1969 that the Justice Department would "wipe out the Black Panther Party by the end of 1969," and the FBI, in coordination with local and state law enforcement, engaged in a vast range of legal and illegal activity to that end.[7]

One frequent strategy was "brown-mailing," the use of the postal service to send fake letters attempting to drive a wedge into the movement. One of the more well-known examples took place in Chicago, where the FBI attempted to invoke a conflict between the Panthers, led by Fred Hampton, and the Black P. Stone Rangers, one of the city's largest street gangs, led by Jeff Fort. In 1969, the FBI forged a letter supposedly from a concerned community member to Fort, declaring that the Panthers had put out a hit on him, and implying he should take action to prevent it. At the same time, the FBI was sending letters to Hampton claiming that Fort was out to kill him. The FBI's own rationale was quite clear, hoping to "intensify the degree of animosity between the two groups," and further cause them to take "retaliatory action" against one another.[8] While Hampton saw through the ruse, such maneuvers undoubtedly added suspicion to the already tense relationship between the Rangers and Panthers, and were intended to prevent Hampton's goals of broader unity between street gangs and political organizations.[9]

Despite their claims to the "free press," the government frequently disrupted the delivery of revolutionary-minded publications, such as the Panthers. The Black Panther newspaper was one of the BPP's most important initiatives. It informed individuals about the Panthers' ideas and goals, and also actions and programs it organized around the country. It was also a source that countered disinformation about the Panthers. The newspaper printed the pictures of known government informants and other individuals expelled from the party for subversive activity. In that sense, the Panther newspaper fit in the Leninist tradition of party papers as a "collective organizer" for the organization. Its disruption inhibited the ability of the BPP to expand and sustain its national organization, particularly in a period when growth was rapid and most new members were totally unknown to the party's central leadership in Oakland. Party Chairman Bobby Seale describes some of the methods used in one particular year:

> In the past, a large number of papers have been stopped, and thousands of issues were received soaking wet...in the process of shipping the papers, the airlines would hold them up in their freighting operations for a week or two...sometimes causing fifty or sixty thousand papers not to show up at all or to show up when they couldn't be sold."[10]

Government officials also made frequent use of infiltrators to disrupt BPP operations and provide the FBI or other national, state or local police agencies with information useful for subterfuge. Snitches were unfortunately rife within the Panther ranks as authorities used every trick in the book to incentivize and cajole individuals into cooperation with the state. They also sent in trained agents provocateurs to join the organization, who would then entrap members in criminal situations, breed disloyalty and attempt to take positions of leadership.

Early Panther snitch Earl Anthony states that there were so many informants and provocateurs that they often informed on each other. Between 1966 and 1975, the Chicago FBI field office alone ran over 5,000 informants, focusing on radical activists and organizations.[11] Federal authorities, among others, had no real scruples about whom they used as snitches. One of the most notorious ever employed was George Sams, a potentially mentally ill, childhood drug addict, with a propensity towards extreme violence. Sams, who had been an informant in Panther offices across the country, used his alleged bona fides with the Oakland leadership to ingratiate himself with the New Haven Panther office. He accused a man, Alex Rackley, of being a police informant. He then proceeded to torture and kill Rackley over his alleged transgressions. Rather than apprehend Sams, Connecticut authorities turned him into their chief witness in a trial that attempted to pin the killing on Panther Chairman Bobby Seale, and stalwart Panther cadre Ericka Huggins. Huggins' husband, John, had already been murdered in a police-instigated row between the Panthers and US, a Los Angeles-based Black nationalist group. Sams' bewildering testimony against Seale and Huggins, when he may have been under the influence of powerful prescription drugs, quickly caused the case to fall apart. But the very fact that the government even attempted such a case demonstrated the lengths to which they would go in order to frame and imprison Panther leaders.

> *Between 1966 and 1975, the Chicago FBI field office alone ran over 5,000 informants, focusing on radical activists and organizations.*

Prison, however, was not enough for police authorities intent on destroying the Panthers. Up and down the chain of command, the state carried out outright assassinations of Panthers, or staged situations whereby they could justify their murder. In April 1968, directly after the assassination of Martin Luther King Jr., Oakland police had attempted to ambush Panther leader Eldridge Cleaver and other Panther cadre. Cleaver and teenager Bobby Hutton—the party's first recruit—were forced into a house during the shootout. Both emerged from the house, fully and partially stripped naked, to show they were unarmed. Hutton

COINTELPRO, police repression and murder were used to disable the radical program of the Black Panthers and others.

came out with his hands up, but the police pushed him, causing him to stumble several feet, before firing 12 fatal bullets into his body.[12]

By 1970, at least 19 Panthers had been killed by police in armed clashes. With clear state and national coordination, Chicago police carried out a targeted assassination of charismatic young leader Fred Hampton while he lay in his bed. Panthers also faced frequent, often daily, harassment from police at their offices, on the streets, and in their homes. They were often charged with criminal activity in attempts to both discredit and harass members. California officials frequently used public disorder statutes to arrest and imprison Panther cadre.

In one particular incident, 23 Panthers who were legally protesting proposed legislation were charged with "disturbing the peace," and hit with $2,200 each in required bail money.[13] Actions such as these were routine in all cities where the Panthers maintained chapters, as were frequent raids and vandalism of Panther offices. Also notable was the harassment of Panther-supporter Jean Seberg, an actress who was driven to suicide by FBI harassment that devastated her personal and professional life.

Years of Freedom of Information Act requests have yielded thousands of files on FBI activities during this period. Some people choose to ridicule FBI efforts for their often amateur nature. Such a perspective omits the deadly seriousness of their operations, and the massive apparatus aimed at "neutralizing" radical activity in the United States. As mentioned above, the law-and-order approach to dealing with revolutionaries and other "militants" was not simply a handy tool for elections. It was a powerful justification for the aggressive campaign directed at physically eliminating organizations dangerous to the capitalist system.

THE LAW-AND-ORDER COUNTERREVOLUTION

A host of politicians on the local and state level took Nixon's lead, building their careers by responding decisively and violently to social unrest. This is how Ronald Reagan got his start as governor of California. In 1964, Mario Savio and the Free Speech Movement at the University of California-Berkeley had ignited a radical student movement, which became a central issue in Reagan's gubernatorial campaign. Reagan lambasted the campuses as hotbeds of communism, where students were encouraged to do drugs, act sexually promiscuous, and riot against authority in a nefarious Soviet plot to take down American prosperity. He too portrayed his campaign as a struggle of the "majority" against a few long-haired campus radicals in league with Black criminals.

In 1965, Reagan accused 35 Black students of putting a switchblade to the throat of a professor, forcing him to admit them to his class.[14] Reagan and other right-wing politicians sought gun-control laws to criminalize revolutionary groups like the Black Panther Party that embraced self-defense and defiantly opposed police violence. People of "good will," Reagan said, had "no reason" to own a gun.[15] As for his own "good will," Reagan promised to meet campus unrest "with bayonets," and police shot and killed student James Rector in the crackdown against anti-war protests. At a rally commemorating his death, police indeed advanced with bayonets and dropped CS gas from helicopters.[16] Nearly all of Reagan's actions were presented in the language of war.

Philadelphia Police Commissioner Frank Rizzo, an open white supremacist—although part of the Democratic Party machine—

strongly endorsed the Nixon-Reagan approach to crime. Rizzo's entire appeal and image was based on his reputation as a "tough cop," and he earned a name nationally by raiding a Black Panther office and forcing its occupants to strip naked in the street. Rizzo's politics and hard-line approach dripped with racism. [17] In his first run for mayor, Rizzo refused to even campaign in Black neighborhoods, and once elected was well known for his frequent use of racial epithets.[18] In 1967, Rizzo's cops violently broke up a large protest by high school students demanding Black studies. When the superintendent described the police action as excessive, Rizzo accused him of "permissiveness."[19] Rizzo declared political, and sometimes actual, war on "bleeding hearts, dangerous radicals, pinkos and faggots."

BUILD UP AND MILITARIZATION OF THE POLICE

This equation of crime with political dissent laid the basis for an enormous buildup of the state's repressive powers. Newly militarized and expanded police forces, as well as national law enforcement and intelligence arms, grew in size and strength. Tougher sentencing laws accompanied the growing size and militarization of police forces. In the 10 years between 1966 and 1976, criminal justice expenditures increased at the rate of five times what it had increased in the previous decade. In the 10 years between 1965 and 1975, the number of police grew by roughly 40 percent nationally.[20] In 1974, $15 billion was spent on criminal justice, 57 percent going directly to police expenditures. On the federal level, President Nixon put in place the Law Enforcement Assistance Administration to funnel large amounts to local police agencies. Between 1968 and 1972, the LEAA received $1.5 billion in federal funds, and in 1972 alone was budgeted to received $850 million. The money was at first distributed through block grants to the states to use how they saw fit, while later involving more federal input.

In Winona, Minn., every police officer was fitted with riot gear, despite the presence of a nearby National Guard armory, where the same equipment could be obtained.[21] Often under the guise of "community policing," many cities placed officers in neighborhoods around the clock. Those like Mayor Rizzo publicly called for police officers on every block.[22] Further the LEAA programs were able to inspire wider funding towards policing and imprisonment from state and local

The growth and militarization of police forces have syrocekted along with mass incarceration.

agencies, with state and local criminal justice expenditures rising 150 percent between 1972 and 1982.[23] The program became notorious for waste and corruption but provided good political cover to a whole host of politicians that aimed to present themselves as tough on crime.

The police did not just expand quantitatively, but shifted in other ways as well, with the formation of paramilitary units to deal with political and social unrest.[24] The Special Weapons and Tactics teams, which have become ubiquitous worldwide, were first formed in Los Angeles in 1968 following the Watts Riots.[25] Future LAPD head Darryl Gates wanted to develop a police unit that could use advanced weapons and military tactics against armed "militants." SWAT's first use came in a raid of the Los Angeles Black Panthers, which led to a major shootout. ☐

Economic and ideological restructuring

"While the productive power increases in a geometric, the extension of markets proceeds at best in an arithmetic ratio. ... Meanwhile, each succeeding winter brings up afresh the great question, 'what to do with the unemployed'; but while the number of the unemployed keeps swelling from year to year, there is nobody to answer that question; and we can almost calculate the moment when the unemployed losing patience will take their own fate into their own hands."

—Frederick Engels,
"Preface to the English Edition of Capital, Volume 1," 1886

THE WAR ON POVERTY

The basic viewpoint shared by both Democrats and mainstream Republicans in the late 1960s was that the U.S. economy was immune to major crises and had unchallenged power in the world. Many declared that the boom-bust business cycle was a thing of the past. The "middle class" had steadily expanded since World War II, unemployment was relatively low, and living standards appeared to continuously increase. While the politicians understood the exclusion of poor Blacks as the country's most explosive social and economic problem, they accepted all the fundamental aspects of the capitalist economic system. The most racist right-wing elements explained Black poverty as a symptom of biological inferiority. But for most liberal and moderate officials, the problem was that Black people had not been adequately trained to fit into the economy.

They advocated for "anti-poverty" programs and minority business set-asides focused primarily on "human capital" approaches: building up the qualities of the individual worker. Under this conception, making "job skills" and job-training programs widely available

The war on poverty

Despite the general affluence of U.S. society in the early 1960s, poverty was still a significant issue, particularly in rural areas and the Black communities of the northern cities. President Lyndon Johnson and other Democrats took notice, still influenced by the New Deal era programs of Franklin D. Roosevelt. They were motivated both by a genuine unease with the extent of poverty in the world's richest nation, and how it threatened unrest.

Following his victory in the 1964 election and a favorable congressional environment, Johnson launched a series of ambitious programs that came to be called "Great Society" programs. They were not limited to poverty prevention, but spanned much of American society. Increased support for artistic and cultural creation, subsidized mass transit, and strengthened environmental and consumer safety regulations all have their roots in this legislation.

The Civil Rights Act of 1964, and Voting Rights Act of 1965 are usually considered part of the broader Great Society era. A massive social movement propelled equality for Black Americans, which dwarfed the organized public support for any other program or issue.

Johnson took particular aim at poverty in selling his broad package of reforms, and created programs under the Office of Economic Opportunity aimed specifically at reducing poverty. Programs focused around early childhood education, community volunteerism, job training, legal assistance to the poor and educational support for low-income students.

Johnson's reforms came amidst increasing unrest over racial inequality, poverty, gender discrimination and opposition to the war in Vietnam. This made many Great Society programs seem like simple band-aids on problems that mass movements were revealing to be very deep and ultimately rooted in the capitalist system. The war on poverty seemed inadequate to address many of these issues, although they did make a difference in some people's lives.

During the decades that followed, most programs were reduced, if not eliminated entirely. They were given the final blow by President Clinton with his "welfare reform."

to Black youth and start-up grants to a few Black entrepreneurs would allow young Black workers to freely and equally compete in the capitalist market. Some additional affirmative action programs would address the effects of discrimination. There was, however, no concurrent jobs program. Inner-city youth were enlisted in job skills programs—many of which wasted time on paternalistic lectures on the importance of showing up on time, or brushing one's teeth—but the government created very few jobs. The assumption even among liberal policymakers who intended to expand the field of civil rights into economic inequality was that private companies would hire the newly trained youth. This was a far cry from economic planning, or guaranteeing full employment (making the government the employer of last resort, when the private sector failed to offer jobs); both these ideas, while floated in different forms throughout the 1970s, were considered too much like socialism. In short, while the government expanded job training and services to alleviate extreme poverty, the burden of finding work remained fundamentally on the poor themselves; once trained, they supposedly would be absorbed into the strong U.S. economy.

Like Johnson before him, Nixon and the mainstream Republican Party viewed targeted social spending as a necessary expense to alleviate pressures from the communities in upsurge. While he devolved aspects of the war on poverty to state control, Nixon went along with the expansion of Social Security and Medicare. While responding with heavy repression to the most radical sections of the Black Power movement, Nixon pledged to promote "Black capitalism" as another variant of Black Power. He argued that the unrest of the inner cities could be quieted by giving militants a "piece of the action" through set-asides for "minority-owned" contractors and hiring on the basis of affirmative action. All this from a known racist! Under pressure from an expanding radicalization and progressive struggles, Nixon also set up the Environmental Protection Agency and the Occupational Safety and Health Administration.

ECONOMIC CRISIS OF THE 1970s

In economic and social policy, the Nixon administration was not worlds apart from its Democratic predecessors. Today's Republican Party operates under the theory of "trickle-down economics"—help the rich get fabulously wealthy and down the road all of society will supposedly benefit. But Nixon and the mainstream Republicans of his era operated as Keynesians, believing the government should manipulate spending and taxes to increase overall spending, freely regulate industries when situations demanded it, and intervene actively in areas that the private sector avoided. The question was: What would happen in an economic crisis when inflation loomed, and the government retreated from social spending?

A series of shocks in the 1970s threw the world capitalist economy into a long slump, in which it was stuck for over a decade. U.S. policymakers, including the architects of the anti-poverty programs, had closed their eyes to the deep stresses within the economy that over the 1970s led to repeated crises. Military spending on the Vietnam War caused inflation to rise, and for the first time the United States ran a balance-of-payment deficit (importing more than it exported). The oil shocks of 1973 and 1979, in which the oil-producing nations demanded much higher payment for their key natural resource, sharply affected capitalist profitability and raised prices on nearly all basic commodities. The decade of the 1970s has thus been dubbed a period of "stagflation," when stagnation and inflation jointly inhibited economic growth and depressed profits.

While the rate of inflation—the rate at which prices go up— rarely rose above 2 percent until the late 1960s, between 1969 and 1973 it hovered around 6 percent every year. Wholesale prices jumped 18 percent between December 1972 and December 1973. In 1974, the rate of inflation jumped to 11 percent and stood at 9 percent in 1975. As prices continued to rise, so did the demand for higher wages to keep pace.[1] Additionally the value of the dollar was falling, making higher wages absolutely imperative for working people to maintain their previous standard of living. Inflation was hardly the only economic problem. Unemployment had ticked up to 5 percent, which in that era was considered quite high.

These twin problems of unemployment and inflation are not easy for the capitalists to resolve, because of what economists call the "wage-price" spiral. To ensure their rate of profit, capitalists will either cut labor costs (leading to lower wages and more unemployment), or increase prices (leading to higher inflation and lower real wages). The problem of inflation is complicated further when the government uses stimulus spending or tax cuts to increase demand or boost investment. Nixon and the Keynesian economists he followed believed these outcomes could be managed by placing government controls on wages and prices—in practice mostly on wages. For a variety of reasons, outside the scope of this book, the plan failed. One long-term result of this era was that it set a precedent of labor unions agreeing to hold down their wage demands regardless of productivity gains, a policy that to this day has helped keep "real wages" stagnant.

In 1974, the economy fell into a full-force recession. Unemployment reached 9 percent in 1975, shocking numbers at the time, and never dropped below 6 percent or 7 percent between 1975 and 1980. Between 1948 and 1967, unemployment had never gone above 6 percent.

During the winter of 1977, fuel shortages resulted in the "idling" of 400,000 workers for varying periods. Economic weakness that winter was further exacerbated by a cold streak resulting in sharp jumps in food prices in some major cities.[2] Investment was low and the depreciated dollar did not stretch as far as it used to. The resulting drop in productive investment was reflected in manufacturing, where the unemployment rate rose to 7 percent in 1977.[3] The net result for working people was a reduced standard of living, and for U.S. society a curtailment of economic growth.

In 1980, the country entered another full-scale recession. Inflation had been accelerating due to a rapidly depreciating dollar. In response to a drastic increase of interest rates by the Federal Reserve System, aimed at stopping a run on the dollar and growing speculation in oil and other primary commodities whose prices were soaring, credit contracted and profits plunged, hurting all industry but especially automobiles and construction.

Waves of plant closures in traditionally strong industries signaled the seriousness of the economic slowdown. The auto industry closed 25 plants between 1979-1980, laying off 50,000 workers. Autoworkers as a whole had already been suffering, with 200,000 (about one in four) on some sort of short- or long-term layoff.[4] Plant closures affected not just the workers directly employed but the entire local economy. A 1974 article in Time magazine had estimated that for every two jobs lost in the auto sector, another three jobs would be lost in local supply industries.[5] This was not just a "normal" recession; the capitalist economy was profoundly changing, and the notion that its contradictions could be forever suppressed by wise bureaucrats turned out to be a myth. One member of Nixon's Council of Economic Advisors retrospectively concluded that any measures aimed at stopping inflation "dead in its tracks" risked "substantial economic and social disarray."[6] In other words, the measures required to restrain a destabilizing speculative boom—which invariably reflects capitalist overproduction—would themselves lead inevitably to a bust—an overproduction crisis.

A newly assertive group of pro-capitalist ideologues, committed to rolling back social programs and the power of labor, crafted an economic program aimed at knocking down all barriers to maximizing profits.

With the Keynesian-influenced ruling-class policymakers having failed so miserably to prevent a major crisis, a vacuum existed for others to step forward. There was a brief flurry of social-democratic proposals, as the AFL-CIO and others called for a new level of government intervention to guarantee jobs or income to all. But given the extent that Keynesian-influenced reformism had been discredited, these never had much of a shot, and a new explicitly pro-business program emerged instead. The politically organized capitalist class pushed a new outlook, inspired by reactionary economists like Milton Friedman, adopted by both parties: Prosperity would be restored through a profound restructuring of the economic model and shredding of the implicit social contract that had governed the previous decades.

Aided by technological advances that enhanced productivity, lowered labor costs and opened up new opportunities for global expansion, the capitalist class aimed to make up for its previous crisis of profitability. As the Keynesian orthodoxy collapsed, a new one took shape based around lower taxes for corporations and the elite; the gutting of the welfare-state social programs; relentless attacks on labor unions; shifting industrial production to low-wage countries in Asia and elsewhere, resulting in deindustrialization at home; and a "new economy" built around the service sector, real estate, high technology industries and finance.

A newly assertive group of pro-capitalist ideologues, committed to rolling back social programs and the power of labor, crafted an economic program aimed at knocking down all barriers to maximizing profits. The government would neither inhibit the rich from getting richer, nor inhibit the poor from getting poorer. In this second Gilded Age, which rivals the first in its extreme levels of inequality, the composition of the working class dramatically shifted. The newly adopted economic philosophy had a direct impact on the permanent crisis within the Black community, and the rise of mass incarceration. Instead of expanding African American entryways into the middle class, these changes brought in new levels of joblessness, inequality and class stratification. The vast majority of Black workers were locked tightly to the low-wage service sector or expelled from the workforce altogether.

EFFECT ON BLACK COMMUNITIES

The economic crisis of the 1970s, extending into the early years of the following decade, hit Black workers especially hard. The wave of auto plant closures demonstrates one aspect of this story. In 1967, a massive uprising took place in Detroit sparked by police brutality, routine discrimination and the lack of employment opportunities. After calling out the National Guard to put down the uprising, the local elites—in combination with the labor leadership—aimed to create more factory jobs to reduce tensions. By 1970, Blacks made up 14 percent of autoworkers. Because Blacks were excluded from more senior positions, hired later and thus often denied promotions based on seniority, they primarily occupied semi-skilled positions, where they comprised 21 percent of the workforce. When the waves of layoffs came, Black workers were the first to be fired.

In the recessions of the 1970s-early 1980s, the pool of unemployed workers continued to increase, and it was disproportionately Black. In 1975, Black unemployment reached Depression-like levels of 22 percent. In New York City, the official measure of Black youth unemployment was an astonishing 86 percent.[7] Numbers in these localities mirrored broader trends in the labor market for Black workers. In 1975, the employment-to-population ratio was only 50.1 percent for Blacks, as opposed to 56.7 percent for whites. This ratio measures the overall rate of participation in the paid workforce and thus leaves out full-time students, stay-at-home parents, active-duty military, and so on. In other words, barely half of all Black Americans of

PHOTO: BILL HACKWELL

Capitalist crises and racism robbed African Americans of economic opportunity, spurring mass incarceration.

working age were employed at the height of the recession.[8] The growth of jobs in the suburbs, areas from which Black workers had been systematically excluded because of racist developmental policies, deepened this trend. The inner city continued to lose jobs, resources and a significant amount of its tax base due to white flight.

Even the small businesses and low-skilled jobs that opened in many cities often did not go to African Americans. In New York City, for instance, waves of immigrants from Latin America, Asia and the Caribbean entered the labor market. Employers opted for those with fewer job protections, who would thus work longer hours at lower pay and with fewer complaints. Over time, immigrant communities built up "niches" in which they used social and familial ties to find job opportunities for those inside their social networks. Immigrants of middle-class background in particular were able to start small businesses. While the working class as a whole is thoroughly multinational, the job market itself remains highly segregated by race and nationality.

The cruel irony of this period in U.S. economic development is that as Black workers migrated to Northern and Western cities, the country's growth sectors shifted elsewhere— towards the nearly all-white suburbs, the low-wage (and racist) Sunbelt, and increasingly, overseas. Further, traditional sectors of the economy, principally the industrial sector, needed less labor as a result of technological innovation. For example, the steel industry in the latter half of the 1970s shifted from the traditional "blast furnace" method of operation to the "minimill." Minimills used scrap steel and the new electric arc furnace, as well as advanced automation techniques, to employ on average 70 percent less labor. Many steel companies that turned towards the minimill faced little or no union pressure to stop them from cutting wages and benefits.[9] Similar trends in a number of manufacturing industries created obsolescence, or surplus, in the workforce. This created an additional barrier for finding work, since capitalists only expand production and create jobs based on expected profitability.

Although the Black struggle knocked down the formal barriers to the "good jobs" in the private sector, these jobs remained closed off due to either racist hiring practices or deindustrialization. The cities' low-wage service sectors—the very jobs from which African Americans had hoped to rise and never look back—grew instead. The struggle of Black workers to find greater dignity in their work emerged formally victorious at precisely the time that the U.S. capitalist economy began to trend towards more degrading, lower-paying work.

The one exception to this rule was in public sector employment. As African Americans began to make their majorities felt in local politics, they opened many avenues for government employment. In this area, hiring practices generally could be subject to more regulations and affirmative action policies, and has ever since served as the most common route for an African American family to earn stable wages and benefits, to enter a strata of the working class often considered "middle class." But affirmative action victories were often limited by the liberals' failure to defend their legitimacy, and the reality that the fight to reapportion jobs to historically oppressed sectors took place amid a declining number of "good jobs."

With the erosion of such work across the nation, however, it was clear by the early 1980s that Black working-class communities had been relegated to a state of perpetual crisis. The same conditions remained that had given rise to the late 1960s urban uprisings. Depression-level rates of unemployment left whole communities and neighborhoods in permanent stagnation, in what amounted to a second society, viewed as veritable "leper colonies" by political elites, and thus walled off from economic incorporation and social develop-

The new economic orthodoxy of neoliberalism revived a type of social-Darwinism—the belief that the economy naturally rewards the 'fittest' and punishes those less deserving.

ment. This provided the "material basis"— the objective socioeconomic reality—for the policies of mass incarceration. As government services contracted, private investors and developers sought more lucrative opportunities elsewhere. When they returned again to the cities, under the name of "urban renewal" or other lofty-sounding labels, they demanded intensified policing and the clearing of neighborhoods deemed otherwise unsuited for investment. Politicians eager to acquire any development whatsoever were quick to oblige. Thus, Black urban communities around the country alternated between neglect on the one side and, on the other, aggressive gentrification schemes enforced through military-style policing.

This was not an inevitable economic development that occurred independent of politics. It corresponded to a new elite consensus, in which liberals abandoned even their rhetorical commitment to tackling poverty, and joined with conservatives like Ronald Reagan to create a mass incarceration regime.

THE 'CULTURE OF POVERTY' THESIS

The gap between the rhetoric of legal equality and the reality of deep racial inequality was plainly obvious. The question was how to explain it. The new economic orthodoxy of neoliberalism revived a type of social-Darwinism—the belief that the economy naturally rewards the "fittest" and punishes those less deserving. Just as this served as the ideological justification of the first Gilded Age of extreme inequality in the late 1800s, it reappeared in the late 1900s to justify the new Gilded Age.

When discussing Black poverty, conservatives largely substituted this sort of cultural racism for the biological racism that had long been used to explain inequality. They said poor Black people were too lazy, uncultured and prone to crime, looking for handouts instead of earning their keep, and coddled by a liberal government that made excuses for their bad behavior.

Of course, such cultural explanations did not always come in such a crude form. They were articulated differently by liberals who proclaimed their desire for racial equality. These intellectuals and commentators, like conservatives, likewise argued that an "underclass" culture severely limited poor Black people's ability to integrate into the economy, but explained this culture in a different way. Some pointed to the damage wrought by slavery on the Black family, while others said the process of deindustrialization eliminated Black male jobs and thus the community's role models. They tied the economic devastation of urban neighborhoods to residents' lack of skills (or "human capital") and their cultural defects. Under this theory, Black people living in "the hood" were predisposed to anti-social behavior and supposedly limited themselves from taking full opportunity of the job market. Such behavior reinforced their own poverty, creating a downward spiral that spanned generations.

Such cultural arguments for poverty, however sophisticated, justified the retreat from affirmative action policies. Reviewing the conservative Thomas Sowell's cultural explanation for poverty, intellectual Nathan Glazer observed in 1984:

> Reluctantly, even Black leaders and civil rights activists seem to be coming to the conclusion that more resources from government in the fight against discrimination ... will do little to affect high rates of illegitimacy, low rates of educational achievement, low rates of participation in the labor force, and other ills of substantial part of the Black minority.

The "underclass" idea was rooted in the work of Daniel Patrick Moynihan, a liberal politician and sociologist whose views directly influenced the war on poverty programs. Moynihan's 1965 report "The Negro Family: The Case for National Action" had argued that slavery had warped the structure of the Black family into a "tangle of pathology" in which women ruled the house, men were denied their rightful place as authority figures and many children were born out of wedlock. This, he claimed, was the root of persistent poverty and

PHOTO: JAMES CARROLL

False theories targeted single motherhood as the cause of rampant poverty.

the "weakness" of Black communities. He urged government action to provide men with jobs so that the Black family could be repaired. His portrayal was blasted by Black activists and revolutionaries, especially Black feminists, and thoroughly debunked by a mountain of sociological literature.

In the face of this reaction to Moynihan, the cultural explanation for poverty was dominated for a time by conservative intellectuals like Thomas Sowell. Sowell argued that "groups with a demonstrable history of being discriminated against have, in many countries and in many periods in history, had higher incomes, better educational performance, and more 'representation' in high-level positions than those doing the discriminating."[10] What then explains Black poverty? Dr. Sowell answered that it clearly was not biology, and therefore had to be a cultural defect: missing positive behaviors and attitudes that allowed other oppressed groups to rise in U.S. society.

William Julius Wilson began writing in the late 1970s to reinvigorate the liberal variant of this cultural explanation. He wrote:

> In the aftermath of the controversy over Daniel Patrick Moynihan's report on the Black family, scholars, particularly liberal scholars, tended to shy away from researching any behavior that could be construed as stigmatizing or unflattering to inner-city minority residents. ... This left the study of ghetto social dislocations to conservative analysts ... so much so that the dominant image of the underclass became one of people with serious character flaws entrenched by a welfare subculture.[11]

But the essence of Wilson's liberal arguments, which came couched in progressive rhetoric and policy prescriptions, was based on many of the same assumptions as Moynihan and the conservatives he criticized. Wilson correctly stated that "the attitudes that many inner-city Black males express about their jobs and job prospects reflect their plummeting position in a changing labor market." But he then went on: "The more they complain and manifest their dissatisfaction, the less desirable they seem to employers. They therefore experience greater discrimination when they seek employment and clash more often with their supervisors when they find employment." Despite the structural and economic arguments that began his argument, his main emphasis was to link "cultural traits with structural realities."[12]

The abstract argument became concrete when Wilson addressed the high unemployment of Black men in Chicago. Reminiscing on the industrial boom era, he recounted how Black American males used to have a more "mainstream" approach to work. Their participation in the formal economy created a healthy network of mutual assistance inside the community, which helped workers navigate a labor market subject to constant discrimination. Once deindustrialization took place, and the factories left, it broke the link between a generation of employed Black people with the youth. Along with the factories, Black communities lost crucial job-hunting skills, and more broadly, a positive community culture. In Wilson's view, inner-city Blacks had since developed a number of coping mechanisms—relying on the underground economy or welfare, while projecting a sense of injustice—which only reinforced the negative perception of these individuals, strengthened job discrimination, and sunk inner-city residents further into poverty.

This view of course came with a left-sounding framework but, like its conservative counterpart, imparted an independent function to behavior and "culture," placing them ultimately at the center of the analysis. Appearing at first glance to be material and historical explanations, they deflected attention away from 1) the persistence of racist hiring practices in the private sector, 2) the government's unwillingness to provide jobs, 3) the inherent drives within capitalism to lower labor costs through wage cuts and layoffs and 4) the long-term uptrend of the unemployment rate. By harping on a so-called underclass work ethic, the implication was that if poor Black people just acted in a way their racist bosses found attractive, real integration into the economy could finally take place.

Wilson's book "The Declining Significance of Race: Blacks and Changing American Institutions," published in 1978, was undoubtedly one of the most influential academic and sociological books of the period. The book drew attention to how deindustrialization was ravaging many Black communities, and noted the growing class division between poor and working-class Blacks with their middle-class counterparts. Studying the Chicago area, he attributed a social and cultural crisis among Black youth to declining manufacturing work. Deprived of not just work, but a supposed work ethic, these "underclass" youths were unable to find jobs, therefore creating a non-stop cycle of poverty.

Wilson was undoubtedly correct about the devastating impact of deindustrialization, but this is hardly the complete story. For one, there were high rates of Black poverty and unemployment that existed even during the industrial boom. Second, the national trend of Black economic decline was severe even in places where industrial work never dominated. And third, in several key cities, such as New York, Black workers had already been concentrated in the service sector.

In fact, the starting point for any serious discussion of Black workers in the U.S. labor market is persistent racism and super-exploitation, together with the long-term inability of the capitalist economy to provide anywhere near full employment. Writing in 1965, the NAACP labor secretary revealed that less than 1 percent of building and construction trade apprentices were Black. Black workers were almost completely locked out of jobs such as "printing pressman, compositors, photo-engravers, stereotypers, paper-handlers, mailers and delivery drivers."[13] A government report revealed:

> Even more important perhaps than unemployment is the related problem of the undesirable nature of many jobs open to Negroes. Negro workers are concentrated in the lowest-skilled and lowest-paying occupations. These jobs often involve substandard wages, great instability and uncertain tenure, extremely low status in the eyes of both employers and employees, little or no chance for meaningful advancement, and unpleasant or exhausting

duties. Negro men in particular are more than twice as likely as whites to be in unskilled or service jobs which pay far less than most.[14]

A 1968 study showed that Blacks made up less than 2 percent of the carpenters' and electrical workers' union, and less than 1 percent of plumbers and sheet metal workers.[15] Another study examined Ford Motor Company employment records from 1918 to 1947. Unlike the rest of the lily-white auto industry, Henry Ford—a Nazi-sympathizer by temperament and ideology—employed a significant number of Black workers. Researchers determined that nearly half of these Black workers were in the grueling, lower-paying foundry jobs, as opposed to just 5 percent of whites. The authors cited a 1940 essay on the foundry working conditions:

> ...In general, foundry occupations are the most undesirable in the industry. Many of them are extremely hot, dirty, and demand exceptional strength. The accident rate is higher in the foundry than any other department in automobile plants. Workers are subject to hazards such as burns from molten metal, flying sparks, and touching heated machinery and metal parts. ... Because of this, white workers do not want foundry jobs. They only take them when nothing better can be secured."[16] One of Ford's own studies admitted, "Many of the Negroes are employed in the foundry and do work that nobody else would do."

Moreover, Blacks were never disproportionately concentrated in industrial work outside of a few cities like Chicago and Detroit. Two authors put it plainly:

> High Black poverty rates, that is, did not result from deindustrialization. Aside from Detroit and Chicago, African Americans did not find extensive work in major cities in manufacturing and were denied the best industrial jobs. Even where Black industrial work was common, service jobs remained the core of Black urban employment. Black industrial workers, moreover, did not earn

higher wages or work more steadily than African Americans employed in other sorts of work. In a sample of fifteen representative cities in 1949, Buffalo, New York, had the largest fraction of Black industrial workers, except for Detroit, but its Black poverty rate was among the highest. In cities with the lowest Black poverty rates, relatively few African Americans worked in industrial jobs.[17]

In 1970, when Black workers reached their highest concentration in industry, only 12 percent of Black men were employed in manufacturing, and as late as 1940, 36 percent of Black men were still employed in agriculture. The decline in agricultural employment was not nearly matched by an equal absorption into industrial work. For Black women, the story was different, as a majority went from agricultural work in 1910 to domestic work by 1940. That number fell to 15 percent by 1970 as more women entered office work, civil rights and affirmative action legislation went into effect, and new opportunities arose in the public sector.[18]

Another review of employment discrimination found that in Chicago, Wilson's subject city, "employers used spatial references as shorthand for racial and class differences within the local labor pool." This was not a matter of work ethic. Discriminating purely on racist grounds, Chicago bosses "were familiar with street addresses corresponding to 'the projects'… and they used their knowledge to practice 'address discrimination' against residents of those areas."[19] In the Los Angeles hotel industry, bosses cared little about job qualifications, opting to exploit the greater vulnerabilities of immigrant Latino workers. The authors examined "the ambiguity in what employers are talking about when they say they are looking for good attitudes, interaction skills, and/or motivation." In reality, "a good attitude may mean someone who accepts the intensification of the labor process without challenging management." "Interaction skills … can also describe an employee's lack of challenge to unfair treatment and work conditions. Motivation may mean the desire to learn new things or it may mean working above and beyond out of fear of losing one's job."[20]

These are just a few examples of what is plainly obvious: Widespread racism has long been the most significant factor in labor market prospects for Black Americans. An examination of unemployment data even at a time of high industrial employment underlines this point. The job situation was bad enough in 1965 that the NAACP labor secretary wrote:

> Negroes now constitute a very large part of the hardcore, permanently unemployed group in American society. In Northern industrial centers one out of every three Negro workers was unemployed for varying lengths of time between 1958 and 1963. ... More than 50 percent of all unskilled Negro workers in the country have been unemployed for substantial periods since 1958.[21]

Labor department statistics in the winter months of 1960-61 revealed that Black unemployment was 13.8 percent as opposed to 7 percent amongst whites. During the same period in Chicago, overall unemployment stood at 5.7 percent; for Black workers this number stood at 17.3 percent. Louisville, Ky., had a 39.8 percent Black unemployment rate when the overall unemployment number stood at 8.3 percent, and in Pittsburgh the ratio stood at 24 percent for Blacks and 11.6 percent overall. These figures can partly be attributed to recessionary pressures, but this just underscores how tenuous employment was for many Black workers. "Last hired, first fired" was essentially a universal concept across the country, and remains so today.[22]

Other studies have shown that even before the Great Depression, there were 50 to 100 percent differences in Black and white unemployment rates in many Northern cities. According to census figures in 1940, at the tail end of the Depression, Black unemployment sat at 9.6 percent. If the loss of the work "culture" caused Black unemployment in the 1970s, why did it not do the same in the 1940s and 1950s after two decades of significant unemployment and underemployment? During this period, moreover, millions of Blacks were emerging from a Southern agricultural sector that had an entirely distinct, non-industrial work discipline. All this refutes the alleged relationship between cultural habits and employment rates. These rates are determined instead by the waves of capitalist development, the supply and demand of unskilled labor, the racist preferences of employers, and as a consequence of the battles waged by workers. William Julius Wilson took a very limited sample and turned it into a vast generalization. He tacked on anecdotal references about an idealized Black middle class to conjure up a supposed golden era of Black culture characterized by plentiful industrial jobs and a strong "Protestant work ethic." Like nearly every other variety of "post-racial" analysis, this one falls flat upon close examination.

Some scholars have shown that Black people significantly dropped out of the lower ends of the service sector because they insisted upon greater pay and dignity at work. The civil rights and Black liberation movements, animated as they were by the promise of real equality, undoubtedly raised the expectations of Black workers for better jobs with better pay. But because capitalist and typically racist employers retained control over hiring and no government effort was made to guarantee such work, only a select percentage of Black people were able to "enter the middle class." Locked out of such middle-class sectors, but determined to avoid the dead-end poverty-wage jobs of the service sector, many Black youth increasingly turned at least partially towards the underground economy. In the final analysis, the problem is not that these youth lacked the proper attitude, or had a "skills mismatch" for the modern economy. The problem was wages: not just the absence of jobs, but the absence of quality jobs.

Wilson argued that poor Blacks create distinct "modes of adaptation" and "subcultural patterns" that departed from the desired norm. Trotting out the conservatives' favored concept—family values—he asserted that concentrated poverty must be examined against the "backdrop of the family." While he steers clear of moralistic or religious genuflection on this subject, the same prejudices about the nuclear family are there. He considers out-of-wedlock pregnancy a negative variable—not just from the perspective of the economic difficulties it presents, but in general as an indicator of the culture of the community.

In short, conservatives and liberals merely reversed the cause and effect in making a roughly similar argument about the "culture of poverty." For conservatives, bad culture created poverty; for liberals, poverty created bad culture, which then became a self-perpetuating element perpetuating poverty. These two trends offered different policy prescriptions to address the "underclass," but both conceptions focused on the behavior of the poor. This view permeated the rhetoric and economic policymaking of Democratic leaders as well as Republicans. It underpinned Clinton's so-called welfare reform, "ending welfare as we know it," and other neoliberal attacks on social programs during his administration, which significantly eroded social services, and magnified the devastation in Black working-class communities. Throughout, Clinton personally promoted Wilson's theories—even while Wilson meekly protested that he had been misunderstood.

Forty years later, little has changed. Poverty remains a third-rail in U.S. politics, merely an isolated "issue" that neither corporate-owned party touches and journalists mention only occasionally. The "common sense" explanation of poverty, even when its victims are presented sympathetically, falsely focuses on the skill sets, lack of education and preparedness of individual employees. Capitalist politicians with national ambitions also consider it politically toxic to talk about inequality, because it is linked immediately with the "race problem"—that is, the disproportionate poverty and overwhelming oppression of Black and Latino communities.

Poverty and inequality are obscured as political issues, moreover, because the educational system, the media and politicians promote the idea that the capitalist economy fundamentally "works." By denying the systemic imperative of capitalism to sharpen inequality and maintain a "reserve army of unemployed," even liberals suggest that the government must only help the "less fortunate" get an "equal opportunity" to succeed. With this pro-capitalist assumption as a starting point, the failure to emerge from poverty and deprivation is explained as a problem of the individual. Conservatives argue that "equal opportunity" already exists, while liberals claim that social programs are sometimes necessary to help the disadvantaged find their way into the economy. But their overall conception of poverty is strikingly similar: It is surmountable with a good work ethic, and those who remain mired in it must have a cultural maladjustment to be "corrected." The other, more sensible conclusion is that inequality will only be resolved through a conscious planning and deployment of society's economic resources.

SUMMARY

With the capitalist class abandoning social programs for their interference with the maximization of profit, it increasingly turned to the criminal justice system to provide the needed "corrections" to nationally oppressed Black and Latino communities in particular. While Moynihan's initial "culture of poverty" report may have been aimed at promoting social programs, in the neoliberal period the same idea was used towards the opposite end: mass incarceration as the state "corrective" to entire communities dealing with chronic poverty and unemployment.

Most importantly, the concept of a self-perpetuating "culture of poverty" played right into the hands of those advocating tough criminalization measures. It closed off discussion of the socioeconomic basis for crime, indeed repudiating such theories. What sort of palliative one prescribes for a problem depends on how one diagnoses it. Having denied the systemic and historical basis for poverty and inequality, which of course could only be resolved with thoroughgoing social transformation, and having focused instead on the "cultural problems," the policies of mass incarceration seemed in step with the "expert" studies of the "ghetto." Finally, the focus on cultural habits lumped all sorts of diverse behaviors—most notably, drug abuse—under the label of a criminal "underclass" culture.

Mass incarceration as conceived and executed by the capitalist state is a means of absorbing and controlling the "surplus population," particularly that sector that has challenged the capitalist system over the past half century, the African American people. ☐

Reagan and state governments on a rampage

The 'war on drugs'

WE have discussed briefly 1) the abandonment of Keynesian economic and social policy, including the war on poverty; 2) the economic shifts, particularly deindustrialization of the 1970s and 1980s that left poor, urban and disproportionately Black communities in a state of permanent crisis; 3) the emergence of law-and-order politics and repression as a response to Black militancy; and 4) the consolidation of a ruling-class ideology that explained poverty and crime as products of cultural defects more than systemic failure. By the 1980s, then, all the pieces were in place for a radically new approach to criminal justice in poor Black communities. This resulted in the massive growth of the U.S. prison population.

The Reagan administration wasted no time in ushering in the new era. His attorney general's "Task Force on Violent Crime" recommended the measures Nixon had suggested in the 1968 "anti-crime" bill, which included the reduction of evidentiary rules by relaxing Fourth Amendment protections, making pre-trial confinement easier, and essentially eliminating the insanity defense. Many politicians around the country developed a patently absurd position that "prison construction" was the most effective tool for reducing crime. The chairman of Reagan's violent crime task force stated:

> The lynchpin of the report concerns significant federal funding for new and renovated state correctional facilities. The problem of available bed space in our state prisons is the single most significant criminal justice issue in the country today. ... The deterrent impact of the criminal justice process rests on the prospect of an available cell. ... If we want to get violent criminals off

the streets—and we most certainly do—we must have a place to put them.[1]

This opening salvo from the Reagan administration set the pace for the 1980s. In the late 1970s, about 100 citizens per 100,000 were incarcerated. In 1980, that number stood at 139; by 1986, it stood at 210; and by 1994, it had reached an astonishing 373 persons per 100,000 citizens.[2] When measuring the total number of individuals "under supervision by adult correctional authorities"—in prison, jail, on probation or parole, we see an increase from roughly 2 million in 1981 to over 4 million 10 years later.[3] In 1984, 34,000 people were serving life sentences; by 1992, nearly 70,000 were locked up for the rest of their lives.[4] From 1984 to 1990, the number of prison guards in state prisons increased by 70 percent—which is no surprise given that some states like California tripled their prison population over roughly the same period.[5] One prison contractor put it plainly: "Prison construction is going crazy all over the country."[6] In just 4 years—1990-1994—Florida doubled its prison construction budget. Between 1983 and 1994, the New York state prison budget nearly tripled.

> *From 1984 to 1990, the number of prison guards in state prisons increased by 70 percent—which is no surprise given that some states like California tripled their prison population over roughly the same period.*

The number of incarcerated people quickly overran prison capacity, and some states started housing inmates in tents or shipping them off to other states. One Texas state legislator revealed how this prison boom was related directly to politics: "Each time the legislature comes in it demands longer sentences. ... So you're always playing catch-up."[7]

The major increase in prison population was of course caused by the tightening of the legal noose, with draconian "anti-crime" bills passing Congress and state legislatures across the country. Driven principally by the fervor of the "war on drugs," first declared by Nixon in the early 1970s, they placed a significant emphasis on adjusting sentencing rules to keep "criminals" in prison significantly longer. The proportion of drug offenders in federal prisons rose from about 23 percent to 54 percent between 1980 and 1990.[8]

Notably, the first mandatory sentencing bill introduced into Congress was brought to the floor by the archetypal "liberal," Sen. Edward "Ted" Kennedy. The anti-crime bills of the era were often sponsored or heavily supported by Democrats, who controlled the House of Representatives during the entire 1980s, up to 1994, and the Senate from 1987 to 1994. In 1984, Senators Ted Kennedy, Joe Biden, Strom Thurmond and Orrin Hatch succeeded in pushing through mandatory minimums in their Sentencing Reform Act. The SRA abolished federal parole and

PHOTO: REUTERS/RICHARD CARSON

Mandatory sentencing and the 'war on drugs' ballooned prison construction.

made existing sentencing guidelines binding on federal judges. That year, Congress also passed the "Bail Reform Act," which was often interpreted as a mandate for courts to simply deny bail to anyone deemed arbitrarily "dangerous." Statistics from 1984 show that federal court districts made little use of pre-trial services, which are designed to help weigh the risks of pre-trial release. In 1986, a district court in Georgia ruled that simply being accused of involvement in "serious" drug trafficking was enough to be held without bail, prior to any conviction.

One Washington, D.C., lawyer told The Washington Post that a 1989 "emergency" mandatory sentencing law would make the District's courts "grind to a halt," with the case backlog.[9] A 1987 article on New Jersey prisons explained: "[P]risoners were being sent to the new prison even before it was completed. Today, there are 545 inmates here, and officials expect that it will be at capacity within a few months."[10] New Jersey officials attributed the boom to "changes in the parole system, requirements for speedy trials and mandatory minimum prison sentences for people convicted of a crime involving a gun or the sale of narcotics near a school."[11]

EXPLOSION OF THE DRUG TRADE

After decades of the "war on drugs," the result has been the incarceration of millions of people, mostly Black and Latino, and the funneling of billions of dollars into weapons contractors and law enforcement agencies. Like the military-industrial complex, this "police-industrial complex" must continuously invent and attack new enemies to prove its worth. But if judged by the enormous volume of drugs sold and used every day, the "war" has been a miserable failure. To the contrary, the 1980s and 1990s saw a massive explosion in the drug trade around the world, in particular in the United States, by far the world's largest drug market. Although described as a "black market," the drug trade is part and parcel of the overall global economy. It was primed to explode by broader changes in international commerce in the 1980s.

The massive increase in global trade in the 1980s, encouraged by the new "free trade" policies, allowed significant amounts of drugs to enter in and out of ports through otherwise legal container traffic. (Those familiar with the HBO series "The Wire" will recognize this scenario.) Additionally, capitalist globalization challenged and destroyed local agricultural economies and industries that could not withstand global competition. In tandem with regional conflicts, this resulted in significant growth of cross-border population flows, while pushing agricultural producers towards more economically "reliable" crops, including illegal ones.[12]

Equally important have been the changes in international banking over the same period, where technological advances have allowed enormous financial transactions based on digital tokens of value rather than hard currency. As one report put it:

> Such funds can be moved rapidly and anonymously and can be traded, exchanged, and cleaned or legitimized via an array of financial instruments such as derivatives and futures. The global financial system has multiple points of access and, once in the system, money can be moved with speed and ease and with a minimum of

interference from regulators. To some extent this was a result of deliberate government choices, with competitive deregulation of financial systems in the 1970s encouraging a more permissive approach to capital, whatever its source. The growth of offshore financial centers and their use for tax advantages by licit corporations established patterns that were soon followed by criminal enterprises, which increasingly use offshore financial centers and bank secrecy havens to hide their money.[13]

These factors contributed to the flourishing of what is now a giant trade, totaling hundreds of billions of dollars a year. The very nature of the drug business makes exact figures impossible, but one 1990 study, used by the United Nations as its baseline for more current studies, estimates illegal drug proceeds in the United States at $97 billion.[14] A more recent U.S. government study from the year 2000 estimated the size of the drug market in 1988 at $154 billion.[15] Cocaine is by far the largest money-maker of all illegal narcotics, generating at least $35 billion in proceeds. This is over three times what is made on marijuana or heroin, the next two largest narcotic money makers, with proceeds totaling around $10 billion.[16] If the American drug business was controlled by one single monopoly, it would fall somewhere between Number 22 and 54 in the Fortune 500. For a more meaningful comparison: the people of the United States spend more on drugs than Coca-Cola products.[17]

RACISM AND THE 'WAR ON DRUGS'

Dr. Stephanie Coontz argues that 70 to 80 percent of drug use goes on outside of the so-called "ghetto." She cites one California newspaper that the average crack addict was a middle-aged, "middle-class," white male—a far cry from the typical picture of the urban "underclass."[18] Yet the vast majority of policing of the illegal drug trade occurs in urban areas that are disproportionately Black and Latino. In turn, these demographics are disproportionately represented in the prison system both as drug users and sellers. Blacks, Latinos and whites, however, use illegal drugs at essentially the same rate. It is therefore impossible to speak about the "war on drugs" without drawing out its racist consequences and underlying assumptions.

In 1986, Congress passed the "Anti-Drug Abuse Act" which contained the now notorious "100 to 1" sentencing disparity between rock cocaine (crack) and powder cocaine. This established a minimum jail sentence of five years for any conviction of crack distribution involving five grams or more. To receive the same five-year sentence for selling powder cocaine required that one sell at least 500 grams. The bill's sponsors utilized the hysteria following the drug overdose of basketball star Len Bias and the panic around drug-related AIDS transmission. It had clearly racist implications, as crack cocaine was concentrated in poor Black communities, while the more expensive powder campaign was associated with white, middle- and upper-class drug users. The bill was finally repealed in 2010, after nearly 25 years of devastating consequences.

When that bill was first enacted, however, it received notable support from the Congressional Black Caucus, indicating the dominance of "law and order" politics among even those who traced their lineage through the civil rights movement. Harlem's congressional representative Charlie Rangel told The New York Times after the bill's signing ceremony, "For the first time, I believe we have a truly comprehensive federal strategy to combat narcotics trafficking and abuse on all levels."[19] By "comprehensive," Rangel meant that the bill included funds for drug treatment. This would become a familiar refrain from liberal Democrats, whose chief contribution to mass incarceration legislation was to add on more money for drug treatment and other "community-based" approaches outside of traditional law enforcement.

Rangel summed up the meaning of "comprehensive" as "eradication abroad, interdiction at our borders, enforcement on our streets, education in our schools, prevention and treatment at home."[20] He called for a federal "drug czar," and even demanded that the Reagan administration enact sanctions (a form of war) on countries where drugs were grown. In 1988, the Omnibus Anti-Abuse Act required five years' imprisonment for simply possessing crack, and expanded mandatory minimums on most drug crimes.[21] When President Reagan later cut some of the funds allocated by the bill, Rep. Rangel opined, "Congress envisioned this program to grow, not to be cut."[22] In other words, the Democratic-controlled Congress, including the leader of the CBC, was calling Reagan "soft on crime"!

THE NEW RIGHT AND THE NEW DEMOCRATS

The New Right coalition headed by Ronald Reagan had its base in the "Sunbelt" region stretching from Southern California to the historic Deep South. The 1970s had produced a number of powerful right-wing movements dedicated to single issues they were against: busing to integrate schools, affirmative action, women's reproductive rights, property taxes and so on. These were mostly bankrolled by "Sunbelt" capitalists flush with cash as the economic growth sectors—oil, aerospace, the defense industry and agribusiness—shifted south and west. This produced powerful economic and political interests with a very different view of the role of government than the "eastern establishment" they often vilified in fake populist terms.

Aggressively pro-free market, these Sunbelt capitalists hated not just high taxes but the principles of taxation and regulation. They connected deeply with the evangelical Christian right wing, which remained the areas' most powerful ideological force. Throughout the 1970s, they battled the aristocratic "liberal" Republicans of the North-east for control of the party. Ronald Reagan emerged as the leader of the party by marrying this insurgent "New Right" with the key economic demands of Wall Street to break labor unions, lower corporate taxes and roll back regulations.

The Democratic Party also underwent seismic changes. In 1968, as the Democrats sought to capture the energy of the anti-war and civil rights movement, they established a quota system that gave additional clout to labor union officialdom, liberal social justice organizations and the Black and Latino petit-bourgeoisie. This institutional shift gave an opening for the presidential runs of Jesse Jackson in 1984 and 1988. Over the 1970s and 1980s, however, a generation of "New Democrats," represented by the likes of Bill Clinton, also arose. Largely based in the Sunbelt areas as well, the Democratic Leadership Conference represented this internal reaction, advocating the abolition of the quotas and functioning as a vehicle for the money interests to reassert their leading role in the party. These New Democrats, while presenting themselves as supporters of civil rights, promoted the basic premises of the conservatives' "underclass" rhetoric. They dropped Keynesian social and economic policy in favor of the Republicans' program. Finally, they presented themselves as even tougher on crime than the Republican Party.

The dominant historical narrative about these New Democrats is that they moved the party to the "center" in order to regain support among white workers and "middle-class" former Democrats who Reagan had successfully co-opted. It is true that these New Democrats aimed to regain the previously "solid" Democratic south that had transitioned to the Republican Party during and after the civil rights movement. But the point about "Reagan Democrats" has been considerably overdrawn, and mistakenly suggests that the population as a whole shifted to the right. The Republicans' ability to attract a higher percentage of white working-class voters has more to do with lower turnout among Democrats, due to disillusionment with the Democrats' anti-labor policies and failures to deliver relief from the stagflation of the 1970s. The country's dramatic lurch towards the right was led by political elites— the middle- and upper-class strata, not poor and working-class whites. Politicians of both parties embraced a new consensus based on aggressive neoliberalism.

The New Democrats claimed that liberal goals could be accomplished through different market-based methods. They demanded a long-term disciplining of the "special interests" like African Americans and union members, who had been central to the Democratic coalition since the New Deal. They were told to stop making "excessive" and "unrealistic" demands, and to give up on the social-democratic aspirations they had entertained in decades prior.

It is worth noting that the DLC's first foray into national politics was a media blitz of Sunbelt states, urging those leaning towards the Republicans to fight it out inside the party rather than switch their party loyalties. The DLC funding patterns tell an interesting story: "Of one hundred DLC Sustaining Members in 1991-1992, fifty-seven were corporations and another twelve were professional or trade associations. The energy, health care, insurance, pharmaceutical, retail and tobacco industries were all represented."[23]

The DLC upheld certain liberal priorities such as national health insurance and made sure to always string along Black organizations and labor unions. But above all, it was defined by its resolutely pro-business stance, and its grounding in "responsible" sections of the ruling class that aimed to limit social spending and regulation. By embracing welfare reform and law-and-order policies, the DLC edged ever closer to the Republican Party.

CLINTON'S 'CRIME BILL' AND GUTTING OF WELFARE

The early 1990s saw the flourishing of "three-strikes" laws on the state level, which gave a life term to anyone who had committed three "serious" felonies. After the State of Washington enacted a three-strikes law in late 1993, within six months similar bills had been introduced in over 30 states. Georgia lawmakers approved a bill giving life without parole to those committing two, not three, offenses in certain categories. As Zell Miller, prominent DLC Democrat from Georgia, said: "If you want three-strikes in Georgia, you'd better join a baseball team."[24] By August 1994, 12 states had enacted three-strikes laws, with South Carolina also enacting a life sentence on the second strike for certain crimes.[25] A Pennsylvania legislator captured the mood: "One legislator wants three strikes and you're dead ... it's Fantasyland up here. I'm trying to get cooler heads to prevail. Whether I'll succeed or not, I don't know."[26]

The fervor on the state and federal level culminated in President Clinton's well-known "Crime Bill," passed in 1994. Clinton had spent relatively little time discussing crime on the campaign trail, apart from promising the funds to put 100,000 additional cops on the country's streets. To avoid seeming "soft on crime," a charge Republicans had frequently used against Democratic candidate Michael Dukakis in 1988, Clinton flew back to Arkansas from the campaign trail to oversee the execution of Ricky Ray Rector, an African American man. Rector had killed a man 11 years earlier at a nightclub, and after negotiating his surrender, killed the police officer with whom he had been negotiating. Rector then shot himself in the head, a bullet that lobotomized but did not kill him. Although severely mentally incapacitated, Rector was sentenced to death and then-Gov. Clinton refused demands for clemency. As a demonstration of his mental condition, Rector told the prison chaplain that he was saving the pecan pie of his last meal "for later." At his execution by lethal injection, the medical staff tried to find a suitable vein for 50 minutes, while witnesses heard Rector moan in pain. Nonetheless, Clinton could deploy the dead body of a Black man as proof positive of his "anti-crime" credentials.[27]

Clinton did not stop there. He called for warrantless searches to be allowed inside of public housing units. After winning the election, he announced a multi-billion-dollar plan to put 50,000 new police on the streets, a "down payment," on his campaign promise. Clinton included a federal three-strikes law and added almost 50 new crimes to be punishable by death in the federal statutes.

In a notorious abrogation of the historic right of a defendant to habeas corpus appeal and due process, Clinton signed the Effective Death Penalty and Anti-Terrorism Act of 1996. The right of a defendant to file an extraordinary appeal is now limited to one year after the end of a post-conviction appeal.

This was not a case of Democrats bending to Republican wishes. "Tough on crime" politics had become a point of ruling-class unity. The crime bill became a competition between Clinton and House Republicans attempting to stake out ground as the truest defenders of innocent civilians against the supposed horde of criminals menacing the country. Clinton made it a primary focus of his first-term agenda, adopting many conservative proposals while successfully co-opting liberals. As Time magazine pointed out, Clinton's proposals had the "distinct ring of traditional Republican Law and Order rhetoric," combined with a "basket of provisions designed to assuage liberal Democrats." [28]

Democrats turned the crime bill into the major centerpiece of the fall elections in 1994. In New York's 14th Congressional District, Carolyn Maloney counted the bill as a key accomplishment while campaigning amongst her super-rich Manhattan constituents. One of the only Black senators, Carol Mosley-Braun, used her support for the crime bill to whip up votes in Southern Illinois, the reserve of Republicans and conservative white Democrats. New York City's Republican Mayor Rudy Giuliani, a man who made his career on flooding oppressed communities with cops, vocally supported Clinton's bill. The liberal editors of The New York Times praised Giuliani's bipartisanship as "courageous." [29]

By adopting historically "hard-nosed" conservative measures, a new liberal orthodoxy arose that attempted to redefine "law and order." Instead of simply meaning more cops and prisons, "law and order" could now include money for drug prevention and treatment as well as "gun control." Essentially no politician in Congress took a stand against the bill on principle. It passed the Democratic-controlled House by a voice vote, and the Democratic-controlled Senate 95 to 4.

The final bill added nearly $10 billion in funding for prisons and $13 billion for additional cops. It eliminated prisoners' eligibility for Pell Grants, sharply reducing their educational opportunities. A

Republican addition to the bill made half of the prison construction funding contingent on states requiring inmates to serve 85 percent of their sentence.[30] This provision essentially stripped parole opportunities for millions of present and future inmates, and guaranteed the prisons would stay full.

Having encouraged the right-wing shift in national politics, the Democrats then lost control of it, as Republicans captured both the House and Senate for the first time since the 1950s. The Democratic control of government had only cemented mass incarceration policies in the U.S. criminal justice system. They prosecuted the "war on drugs" with equal vigor, insisting hypocritically on more drug prevention programs while advocating for mandatory sentencing and three-strikes rules.

Another shocking element was funding for states to run "bootcamp" style youth "intervention" programs. As one national newspaper put it, "All shock camps nationally are built on the military model, with emphasis on discipline and a large dose of humiliation, in the belief that tougher prisons can shock young criminals into shape." New York's pioneering "shock" program had the following daily schedule:

> [G]et up at dawn for calisthenics and a mile run, work all morning at a lumberyard, attend afternoon counseling and academic sessions, partake of all meals in silence, speak only when spoken to and endure more physical training before lights out at 9.[31]

The program was strong on symbolism, appealing to the "culture of poverty" idea popular in both conservative and liberal circles. But it was short on effectiveness. The Washington Post noted "the recidivism rates for shock graduates and regular parolees in New York become almost identical at four years out."[32] It is easy to understand why. The central problem of youth crime was always economic, not cultural. One graduate sarcastically explained: "All I got out of shock was how to fold my socks and keep myself clean." Another recounted that after completing the program, his new state-sponsored job required him to work on a cleaning crew making $20 a day, significantly less than his former drug income. He quit after two days.[33]

CRISIS IN BLACK LEADERSHIP

Liberal Black and Latino legislators were part of this overall trend within ruling-class politics. They embraced the law-and-order rhetoric that increased prison budgets and law enforcement, although these policies helped criminalize the very communities they represented. Why? On one hand, there were very real problems of crime and drug abuse, stemming ultimately from racial discrimination and chronic unemployment. While many community members instinctively hated the police because of their racist and anti-worker character, others demanded more cops and stricter criminal enforcement—either for ideological reasons or sheer exasperation. No longer under the pressure of the social movements of the previous decades, leading liberal politicians in oppressed communities generally upheld the bourgeois intellectual theories that emphasized "underclass" culture as the basis of crime. The Congressional Black Caucus said mass incarceration policies would remove problem elements from the community, and adjust "bad behavior" in others, provided that funding for drug treatment was included in anti-crime measures. While they offered these "liberal" additions, Democratic politicians as much as Republicans united around the two major "anti-crime" bills that jump-started the mass incarceration epidemic.[34]

No longer under the pressure of the social movements of the previous decades, leading liberal politicians in oppressed communities generally upheld the bourgeois intellectual theories that emphasized 'underclass' culture as the basis of crime.

The Congressional Black Caucus had been central to initial opposition to the crime bill, but eventually lined up behind it with near unanimity (only six dissenting). Kwesi Mfume, then CBC chairman, defended this under typical "compromise" grounds. The CBC's support for Clinton's draconian crime bill also reflected the growth of a more conservative trend in Black politics in the 1990s. Clinton's New Democrats spoke to a particular layer inside the Black community by offering scolding, moralistic speeches about cultural degeneration. Most notable was a 1992 speech at a conference of the Rainbow Coalition, in which Clinton spoke out against "Black-on-Black violence." Speaking in 1994 before the National Baptist Convention, the country's largest Black religious organization, Clinton attributed persistent poverty in the Black community to a "crisis of values." He insisted on greater "personal responsibility," laying on thick the culture-of-poverty rhetoric. At the height of the civil rights and Black liberation movement, few white politicians could have gotten away with such a presentation, but on this occasion and many others during the 1990s it received considerable applause.

The popular resonance of such arguments is entirely understandable in areas experiencing high levels of violence and drug use. But the existence of such problems does not make inevitable the mass incarceration policies used to address them. That these were widely upheld in the Black political establishment reflected not only the desperation of their constituents, but also the growing strength of a middle-class conservative trend in the Black polity. More fundamentally, it demonstrated the extent to which the established "Black leadership"—regardless of the social movement origins of many—had become entrenched inside and ultimately beholden to the Democratic Party. As the party moved to the right, they moved with it.

The ruling-class strategy of carrot-and-stick—co-optation and severe repression—had by the early 1980s left Black radical organizations, and the left more generally, in a severely weakened state. It also opened a wider political space for socially conservative organizations and ideas to grow among African Americans more generally.

Liberal government programs, as we have discussed above, failed to eradicate poverty. Affirmative action had indeed helped many African Americans enter higher education and white-collar work, but it did not alter the underlying low-wage job market in which the vast majority of Black people were forced to survive—if they were lucky enough to get jobs at all.

The rightward turn of many white liberals—and elite "respectable" opinion in general—clearly influenced many Black political leaders. As a result, "self-help" ideas came to the fore, expressed in different forms (from neoliberal to nationalistic), which had not been widely prevalent for decades. "We must find ways to do for self," the NAACP's new chairman Kwesi Mfume told The Washington Post in early 1997.[35] Many prominent Black churchgoers, one commentator observed, enjoyed middle-class lifestyles, "do not have an anti-poverty agenda and may have a derogatory view of those who are still in poverty."[36] The October 1995 Million Man March in Washington, D.C., reflected a significant resurgence of the Nation of Islam. Sharp critics of white supremacy and imperialism, the Nation of Islam was, however, socially conservative, and between 1995 and 2000 pursued a strategy focused on restoring "family values." In step with leading Black Christian organizations, the NAACP, and many academic voices, the NOI identified cultural decay as the key source of poverty. Though the NOI had a different answer to poverty—buying from Black businesses and reducing the dependence on white America—their diagnosis overlapped considerably with mainstream bourgeois opinion.

Space does not allow a full exploration of the debates and contradictions within Black politics of the period. But it is worth noting the growing cadre of Black neoliberals, and the religiously based revival of personal responsibility and self-help rhetoric. This created fertile ground for mass incarceration policies, and allowed them to be enacted as "color-blind" despite the disproportionate and destructive impact on poor Black communities.

SUMMARY

The economic crisis of the 1970s and early 1980s created the space for a new ruling-class political consensus around lowering taxes, "reforming" welfare (forcing recipients to work or starve) and aggressive incarceration, among other issues. Capitalists, as a class, aimed to take home more of their profits, and reasserted their right to lead society without government regulation. They promoted a pull-yourself-up-by-your-bootstraps worldview—as false in the second Gilded Age as in the original one. They cast welfare recipients and "ghetto" residents as lazy, attributing crime, including drug use, to defects of character. This is often referred to broadly as neoliberalism, which can be boiled down to one basic idea: more wealth and power for the top. Under this ruling-class consensus, the notion that poverty could be addressed through social services and movements towards higher wages found little support.

This convergence within ruling-class politics led to the passage of major crime legislation in the 1980s and 1990s, which resulted in skyrocketing imprisonment among Black working-class communities. "Centrist" Democrats, seeking the power and resources of Sunbelt capitalists, appealed to middle-class sectors that both feared and scapegoated "the ghetto" as the cause of the country's economic and social problems. Taking the Black vote for granted, which would be mobilized regardless through Black middle-class organizations and the party machines, top Democratic figures went to great lengths to show they could be just as tough on crime as Republicans. A moderate, and sometimes conservative, trend among the Black political establishment made it possible for the Clinton administration to carry out this racist program with a non-racial face.

Taken together, it is clear that mass incarceration was and is a class project. While Republicans take the brunt of liberal criticism for "tough on crime" law-and-order policies, the Democrats are just as complicit, and in some cases the key link, in the cornerstone legislation of the system of mass incarceration. This system targets mostly poor and working-class communities, disproportionately Black and Latino, and is furthered by widespread racist assumptions amongst whites.

However, it has also been deployed by Black politicians, not on the basis of racist rhetoric, but on shared bourgeois assumptions about the root causes of poverty. For those seeking to overturn mass incarceration, it is insufficient—to say the least—to single out racist Republicans. The real onus belongs on the capitalist class and their political representatives from the federal to the local level. They crafted the mass incarceration regime to deal with the permanent economic and social crisis in the hood, "disciplining" impoverished communities with military-style policing and incarceration. □

Problems and Solutions

Debunking bourgeois theories of 'crime'

AS liberal sociologists reintroduced and repackaged the "culture of poverty" thesis in the 1970s and 1980s, a complimentary theory was developed in the field of criminal justice. While such bourgeois intellectual trends do not in and of themselves explain the mass incarceration dynamic, or any historical phenomenon for that matter, they are important to examine. "Expert" opinion sets the limits of what is considered "respectable"—and conversely "extreme"—in national politics. Therefore, a movement against mass incarceration must not only expose the racism, inhumanity and devastating consequences of such policies. It must also tear down the ruling-class theories that justify mass incarceration. This chapter suggests a few lines of argument to do precisely that.

'BROKEN WINDOWS THEORY' AND 'ZERO TOLERANCE'

A leading intellectual force in criminal justice doctrine in the 1980s and 1990s was James Q. Wilson, a specialist in urban social policy. Wilson, who considered himself a liberal, began his theory from the very sunny premise that many of a human's best attributes—sympathy, reciprocity, fairness—are natural and not "created" by society. This is all reasonable enough, based on the recognition that humanity has the capacity for a decent or "moral" society. He rejected the view that human beings are "naturally" selfish and that only the fear of government keeps us from robbing and killing each other. Instead, Wilson argued that civil society and the government transmit and encourage negative and anti-social behaviors.

But the further elaboration of Wilson's social theory reveals how rather innocuous, even optimistic, ideas can be mobilized to reactionary ends when translated into the imperatives of the capitalist state.

Wilson and his co-thinker George Kelling originated what became the "broken windows" theory of crime control, which initially appeared in the liberal *Atlantic* magazine. The broken windows theory held that key to crime reduction was for the police to focus on nuisance crimes, like vandals breaking windows. By paying close attention to the violations that most people consider relatively minor, the state will make clear that criminality of any sort will not be tolerated. The argument is that by maintaining a stable and safe environment, the government signals that the area is monitored, thereby discouraging crime. It called for a massive police presence and a display of force to alter the social environment and expectations of the population, even if this could be expected to violate basic civil liberties.

The first major focus for the broken windows theorists was to clamp down on graffiti culture, which was taking New York City and other urban centers by storm, as primarily Black and Latino youth converted the physical landscape of the city (trains, walls and so on) into their landscape.

This phenomenon provoked outrage from ruling-class liberals and conservatives alike, who preached about the necessity to maintain the "order" and image of the cities that the "average" person expected. A sneering contempt for the culture of Black and Latino youth often was barely concealed, as well as racist and class assumptions about what was "normal" and who was "average."

Nathan Glazer, an influential Harvard sociologist, on his way to becoming a neoconservative, wrote:

> Even if graffiti, understood properly, might be seen as among the more engaging of the annoyances of New York, I am convinced this is not the way the average subway rider will ever see them, and that they contribute to his sense of a menacing and uncontrollable city. The control of graffiti would thus be no minor contribution to the effort to change the city's image and reality.[1]

Glazer argued that graffiti artists cannot be reasoned with on moral grounds, because they have the audacity to consider themselves legitimate artists. Thus, the state should protect the alleged "societal norm" that abhors graffiti and clamp down. Apparently, it was beyond consideration to think that the perspective of "average subway riders" with respect to such public art, and the social norm, could be changed. Such "experts" argued that minor crimes like graffiti, if permitted, would encourage the sense that the government is not in control.

Over time, this approach acquired the name "zero tolerance," a slogan that politicians from both parties proudly upheld. In everything from school discipline to felony sentencing guidelines, the argument went that strong mandatory punishments, starting with small violations, would correct and discourage anti-social behavior. Correctional methods must be employed as necessary. Laws making stiff punishments and sentences mandatory were designed specifically to prevent individual authority figures from taking into account one's context or previous history. The era of the "slap on the wrist," policymakers proudly declared, was over (although not for bankers, of course!).

Much of the zero tolerance ideology could be found in the old "permissiveness" argument of the Nixon administration. It also shared many underlying assumptions with the "culture of poverty" theories that explained the problems of the hood by pointing to their distinct cultural roots, and specifically the failure to conform. The same logic was used to push through welfare reform, based on the spurious argument that the existing welfare system encouraged laziness and dependence in contrast to the "normal" work ethic exemplified by the country's middle class. Such criminal justice theories explicitly reject the idea of poverty and inequality as root causes of crime. In fact, to this day, mainstream criminology tends to consider these factors relatively unimportant, or completely inconsequential.

What such theories take as a given—the "social norm"—is precisely what must be defined and exposed.

A MARXIST ANALYSIS OF THE LAW AND CRIME

If the notion of an "underclass" culture fails to explain the social phenomena of violence, drugs, and so on, how can revolutionaries and activists present another analysis?

For one, the whole notion of crime must be challenged and examined. There can be no universal theory for "crime," because it is defined by the shifting boundaries of the law and law enforcement, and the objectives of a given ruling class. What is a crime at one time, or in one place, may be considered merely a minor problem, or none at all, in another. Moreover, any attempt to give an overall theory of "criminal behavior" must group together a whole range of things—from theft, to drug use, to sexual assault to corporate fraud—that in fact have different roots and explanations.

Karl Marx argued that the law is fundamentally an instrument for the rule of one social class over another. Under capitalism, the law's central purpose is to protect private property and the right to accumulate profit. As an example, some of the most gratuitous forms of theft—daily exploitation at the job, usurious interest rates, bank bailouts—are considered completely legal, and the perpetrators are in fact rewarded. One can receive a stiff sentence for robbing a bank; but when a bank systematically robs society as a whole, no one goes to jail.

> *Under capitalism, the law's central purpose is to protect private property and the right to accumulate profit.*

The same is true in the "war on drugs." Despite HSBC's admission of having laundered billions for the largest drug cartels, all the banking giant paid was a fine. Street-level dealers are, as a rule, not treated with such leniency. This class function of law enforcement is demonstrated in eviction proceedings; the cops come to remove and even arrest the tenant instead of going after the landlord depriving a family of the basic right to housing. In a strike, likewise, police come to subdue and repress the workers, while protecting the safe passage of scabs. In both cases, the private property of the landlord and business is sacrosanct, and whoever challenges that is subject to repression and criminal prosecution. As a last example, consider the police repression and sabotage of political challenges from below—from the early labor movement, to the Black liberation movement, to the recent Occupy movement. In no way is the law a neutral force, dispensing "justice" equally in every direction.

POVERTY AND INEQUALITY

Some progressives focus purely on poverty as the cause of crime. While inequality and the inherent inability of the capitalist economy to provide full employment is a suitable starting place for a discussion of crime, it is not the whole story. One must consider the political function of law enforcement, and why certain behaviors are criminalized in one time or place but not in others. Why, in other words, did "crimes" such as graffiti writing, hopping a turnstile, smoking a joint, or fighting in school warrant a specific repressive state intervention in one community but not in another community or time period?

Moreover, while there is a link between poor economic conditions and crime, poverty in itself obviously does not mean someone will engage in behavior defined as criminal. Nor does crime exactly mirror economic trends. In the 1960s, for instance, "crime" increased nationally across nearly all categories despite the relatively strong economy and low unemployment. Cities and states sometimes experience temporary spikes in violent crime—like robberies—that are not always linked to overall economic trends. For trends in violent sexual crimes such as rape, poverty and the rate of unemployment are unlikely to serve as useful predictors.

In addition to poverty—that is, the condition of being poor in absolute terms, it is often more useful to examine inequality—that is, relative levels of deprivation. In previous stages of human development, for instance, when societies experienced greater deprivation in absolute terms, it did not follow that there was more crime. Marx explained in "Wage, Labour and Capital":

> A house may be large or small; as long as the neighboring houses are likewise small, it satisfies all social requirement for a residence. But let there arise next to the little house a palace, and the little house shrinks to a hut. The little house now makes it clear that its inmate has no social position at all to maintain, or but a very insignificant one; and however high it may shoot up in the course of civilization, if the neighboring palace rises in equal or even in greater measure, the occupant of the relatively little house will always find himself more uncomfortable, more dissatisfied, more cramped within his four walls.

Confirming Marx's argument, the existence of sharp inequality is generally a greater predictor of "property crime" than poverty. This may be because inequality enhances the opportunities for theft, or because it breeds a deeper resentment within those at the bottom of society—or both.

While economic indicators—such as unemployment, inequality, or poverty—must frame a discussion of crime, they cannot account for all the shifting trends in human behavior. A materialist analysis, rather than crude economic determinism, focuses on the totality of social and economic relations that give rise to certain ideas, attitudes, cultural responses and behaviors. Modern U.S. capitalism is not just built on economic inequality; it is built on racism and national oppression, the degradation of women, and the privileging of the patriarchal nuclear family as a unit of reproduction. Capitalism is likewise a mode of production based on instability, the boom and bust cycle, and simultaneous construction and destruction in a continuous drive to maximize profit. To meet and if possible best the competition, the capitalists must shift investments and squeeze and often eliminate workers. They must put a monetary value on more and more elements of life, and create new needs whose satisfaction comes with a price.

The vast majority of society has no control over this process, and merely tries to create a modicum of stability while the ground beneath is always shifting. Meanwhile, people are bombarded with advertisements, messages and values of hyper-consumerism, alienation, and individualism. The result is never-ending psychological and economic stresses, social pressures and conflict, which are especially acute for poor and working people. Some turn to drugs and alcohol as a way to escape; others turn to the illegal economy where the formal economy offers bare subsistence, if that. In both cases, the law functions to stigmatize and institutionalize these sectors of the population whose conditions of existence best demonstrate the failings of the system.

CRIME STATISTICS AND TRENDS

Only from this broad view of the law can we begin a closer study of crime. Nearly every discussion about this subject is hobbled by the challenges of crime statistics. Crime statistics are often aggregated so that many different crimes of various levels of seriousness are lumped together. They are subject to constant and contrasting

Attica, above, and other prison rebellions were a response to growing incarceration and brutality in the wake of the 'war on crime.'

political pressures as mayors and police commissioners distort and bend statistics to meet their needs of the moment—often to show that existing policies are working or that more police presence is needed.

For nearly every study that attempts to explain the rise and fall in crime rates, there is another that directly contests it. Some have come to the conclusion that crime statistics are so routinely manipulated, consciously or otherwise, that they are practically useless. Each of the few broad indices for crime has its own particularities. For example, the Uniform Crime Report (UCR) and National Crime Victimization Study (NCVS) are based on self-reporting by police departments, and jurisdictions often collect data differently. Only very broad trends can be identified with a degree of confidence. At the very least, studying the problems of crime statistics can tell us quite a bit about the overall problem of how society understands crime.

In the most recent period of U.S. history—which covers mass incarceration—the link between poverty and crime appears to be rooted most specifically in the shifting dynamics of the labor market, and the rise of the drug industry as the foundation of an expansive underground economy. There is a clear link between the decline in wages and job opportunities, combined with the new opportunities in the illegal drug economy, that account for both increases and declines in "crime rates" from the late 1960s to the present.

In the earlier discussion of the economic crisis of the 1970s and early 1980s, we reviewed how deindustrialization, the erosion of social spending and affirmative-action policies, combined with pervasive employer discrimination, and the transition to a service-based economy sharply restricted employment opportunities for African Americans. Absent a real jobs program, and with private capital permitted to make all decisions related to employment, finding a job was often reduced to "who you know" and the "preferences" of bosses. In some cities, immigrants, more vulnerable because of their status, filled many of the low-wage service jobs. Other immigrants arrived with greater access to capital, and built specialized economic markets that distributed jobs within their own niches based on kinship. But immigrants are not to blame for inner-city poverty. Even in places where undocumented immigration was a minor factor and did not put downward pressure on wages, African American communities were still plagued with unstable and low-end job opportunities.

As these economic trends took hold in the 1970s, both property crime and violent crime rose fairly steadily, peaking in 1980. While the data for the 1970s is less clear, there is an indisputable relationship between the emergence of the crack trade and crime in the 1980s. "Crime rates" rose overall from the beginning to the end of the decade, but notably it appeared to be falling in the early 1980s until the explosion of the crack epidemic. In many states, there was a notable boom in violent crime between the mid-1980s and 1994. One study, examining 705 counties from 1979 to 1997, found that property and violent crime increased over the 1980s before declining from 1994 to 1997.

During the period crime increased, the average wage for a man with no college education decreased 23 percent. As the study went on to show, these dismal wage patterns and the crime patterns were "almost the mirror image" of one another.[2]

'UNDERCLASS CULTURE' OR JUST GETTING BY?

Other studies have shown that those in the informal and illegal economy often work off and on in the formal and legal economy, or do both at once. A study of drug dealers in two Manhattan neighborhoods found that one out of every four dealers had some sort of legal income, ranging between 7 percent and 33 percent of their income.[3] A national survey found that 33.8 percent of those surveyed both worked legally and committed "income-producing crimes." Drug dealing is often used to create start-up capital for above-ground businesses; on the other side, legal work can create social contacts that facilitate illegal work.

The move between legal and illegal work often follows its own logic, based on available economic opportunities, not cultural deviance. Moreover, one's choices are often determined by the opportunities available at a moment in life during the "school-to-work" transition. Much has been written about "skills mismatch," in which the education system does not provide the skills for employability. But the problem is deeper than that. What sort of jobs are available? One 1990 study of drug dealers in Washington, D.C., found that the net mean income for these dealers was $1,799 while $1,046 was the mean for legal work.[4]

Several studies, including many from the early 1990s, attempted to find the "reservation wage" at which drug-dealers would give up criminal activity. They settled around roughly $30 per hour—a "middle class" wage generally unattainable in the service sector. A study of inner-city young men in Boston in 1989, when the economy was generally doing well, found that a full 69 percent believed they could make more money on the street.[5]

Wages are not the entirety of the story, of course. With illegal work, there are no benefits, and far greater risks—over the years, a street-level dealer is all but assured of facing jail time at some point. But even this must be weighed against a variety of other factors, and one should not assume that a dead-end low-wage job where one interacts with racist bosses or customers is a vast improvement. There may well be greater opportunities for advancement in the underground economy—and greater ability to find work—than in the low-wage service one, especially once an individual has a conviction on their record. Given the huge and durable market for illegal drugs, the industry also offers a type of "job security."

Beyond economic calculations, there are several "social" issues involved in the decision to enter the underground economy. For example, as more peers enter the drug game, the social stigma around incarceration lessens. Rather than perceiving it as deviant behavior, individuals believe they are "doing what they have to do," engaging in a form of necessary work, not "crime."

Moreover, considering that the pursuit of individual wealth is the foundation of the national culture, drug dealing appears to offer greater enrichment than working at McDonald's. The latter not only offers low wages but also carries a social status that is demeaned in popular culture. At the same time, organized crime and the Mafioso culture is also widely celebrated in television shows and movies—provided the main characters are of European descent. Every aspect of our society encourages conspicuous consumption. While some blame newly rich hip hop artists for this "bling bling" culture, few ever blame Donald Trump or free-spending Wall Street executives. From this perspective, those engaged in drug dealing are not "deviants" at all, but conforming to the values and aspirations promoted by society at large. The urge to get "crazy money" not only motivates drug dealers—it motivates huge numbers of college graduates to pursue a masters in business administration.

All of this invalidates a central premise of the culture of poverty theory: that having a formal job creates different values. Cultural values may have little or nothing to do with one's entrance into criminal activity, which can result from one's survey of opportunities and challenges. Such decisions can be made out of immersion in the dominant social and cultural values.

The link between participation in the underground economy and the lack of economic opportunities in the above-ground one casts significant doubt on the whole concept of an "underclass" culture. The prevalence of combining legal and illegal work also shows that skills mismatch is an overrated factor in determining unemployment. In fact, high unemployment, low wages and the lack of advancement opportunities are the key factors in one's decision to bypass the legal labor market.

THE SO-CALLED 'DISINTEGRATION' OF THE FAMILY

The idea that inner-city Black communities have an "underclass," criminally inclined culture is often linked to the so-called "disintegration" of the Black family. Analysts point to higher rates of out-of-wedlock children, the leading role played by women in many

Black families, and the absence of male role models to make their case. They refer to these as "pathologies"—deviations from the norm, which, like diseases, produce a whole assortment of negative consequences. First and foremost, it must be stated that the very concept of the "normal" family is based on a patriarchal bias. Secondly, to the extent that two-parent homes are less likely to be in

George Jackson, a Black Panther and prison hero, promoted a revolutionary program to solve society's ills.

poverty, it is not because of distinct cultural values but because wages are so low that multiple adult incomes are necessary for family survival. Furthermore, there are several important tax codes, and access to job-related benefits, that privilege the married nuclear family over other sorts of family arrangements. The U.S. nuclear family is reproduced and upheld as a superior economic unit because of this social context, not because of any inherent superiority over other forms.

Let's examine this further. While single-parent households in poor communities are often demonized, there is no concomitant demonization of well-off working women who are raising their children on their own. Few objections are raised since, after all, they are able to afford quality housing, health care, childcare and vacations, and can hire assistants in special circumstances. If these basics of a decent upbringing were guaranteed by society for all children, single-parent households would be understood in a completely different way. Black female unemployment is roughly two times white female unemployment and among married women is 2 percentage points higher. Eliminating the discrimination against women, and Black women specifically, would thus rapidly undercut the idea of Black communities suffering from particular "pathologies."

In discussions of the so-called underclass, the terms "single-parent household" and "female-headed household" are often used interchangeably. Having a family with a strong female head is considered "deviant," while male single-parent households are rarely scrutinized.

To be sure, these families are rarer, but it reveals the sexist assumption that a family must have two parents, headed by a man.

Studies from the 1980s revealed that most Blacks living in poor single-parent households were also poor prior to their family splitting.[6] In addition, there are clearly millions of impoverished nuclear families, dealing with long-term unemployment, foreclosure, and so on. All this should temper generalizations about the relationship between the form of one's family and poverty. In 1992, two out of every five impoverished children lived in homes with two parents.[7]

The image of promiscuous unmarried Black women must be challenged on both anti-racist and empirical grounds. Contrary to the popular image, research showed that birth rates among unmarried Black women actually fell by 13 percent from 1970 to 1990. Because birth rates among married Black women fell by a larger 38 percent over the same period, only the proportion of Black children in single-mother households rose. But this hardly amounts to the stereotypical image of single Black women and the Black family promoted by bourgeois criminologists, politicians and—unfortunately—certain political forces inside the Black community.

There is also the stereotype, often brought up in these discussions, that unmarried fathers (and especially Black fathers) are entirely negligent of their children. Supposedly this absence of responsible men is responsible for crime. Without neglecting the unbalanced burdens of child-rearing that are placed on women, in nearly all contexts, married and unmarried, this too must be challenged. A 2003 study found that at the child's third birthday, 74 percent of unmarried fathers saw their child at least one day out of the month, with 45 percent reporting that they spent an hour or more with their child on a daily or nearly daily basis. Paternal involvement in a child's life correlates to whether the parents are romantically involved or living together, not marriage per se.[8]

Revealing the absurdity and biases of "underclass" theories, historian Stephanie Coontz looked at the family lives of soldiers and police officers, whose values are typically celebrated in mainstream coverage:

> "[W]e know, for instance, that families whose breadwinners are police officers or who serve in the military have much higher rates of divorce, family vio-

lence, and substance abuse than do other families, but we seldom accuse them of constituting an 'underclass' with a dysfunctional culture; more reasonably we relate these problems to work stresses and other situational or structural issues."[9]

In summary, the "underclass" ideologists vastly overplay the scale of out-of-wedlock children, and attach undue significance to it in the discussion of poverty. While changes in the family structure are connected to broader economic and social policies, it is misguided to view these changes as central to poverty with their own power to make and unmake the financial well-being of any individual who chooses to (or not to) get married. Moreover, to the extent that the choice to not marry damages one's economic opportunities, that is an indictment of the social system, not the individual.

CONCLUSION

The false "culture of poverty" rhetoric and all its attendant social policy proposals are of great import to mass incarceration. If the real issues driving individuals' participation in the underground economy are limited wages and socioeconomic opportunity, the implications are clear: We need not prisons, but good jobs, guaranteed incomes and a different organization of the economy.

Furthermore, this understanding of crime demonstrates the need to separate serious drug addiction (especially with respect to crack, heroin, crystal methamphetamine, and so on) from "crime." Instead of understanding these as symptoms of a cultural predicament, they must be treated as public health issues, and understood as a broader indictment of society's failings. There is no point in sending drug users to jail and little hope in temporary treatment centers if afterwards addicts are left to fend for themselves in the same social conditions that produced their initial addiction.

There is a transparent hypocrisy in a culture that exalts the mindless maximization of profit but then wags its finger at street-corner drug dealing. The fact that a massive legal apparatus exists to catch even the tiniest drug dealer, while Wall Street firms that ruined millions of lives merely pay inconsequential fines, is a crime in itself. The real solution to crime of all types is not just jobs, or government programs, but a different type of society, which directs the collective wealth, knowledge and productive capacity first to satisfy our collective human needs. Such a society would create the basis for a new culture to emerge totally anathema to the every-man-for-himself, get-rich-or-die-trying, Pablo Escobar-Goldman Sachs capitalist value system. □

What alternatives to mass incarceration?

THIS book comes at a time when incarceration policies are still riding high, with over 7 million people, mostly Black and Latino, under the purview of correctional services of some sort. At the same time, there are more demands than ever to end or dramatically reform this system. In particular, the "war on drugs" has gained a number of critics from sections of the ruling class (mostly liberal and libertarian). A reduction of the prison population is the purported goal even by the pro-business lobby ALEC, the very organization that drafted key laws that fueled the mass incarceration and recruited the lawmakers to pass them!

This should immediately raise red flags among progressives and revolutionaries. It shows the need for an alternative vision, centered on the needs of working-class and oppressed communities, to counter the mass incarceration regime. In the absence of such an alternative, our choices will be confined to either continued mass incarceration or a "reform" agenda that really aims to reform capitalist and national oppression.

For one, the superficial agreement on scaling down the prison system from groups like ALEC shows the danger of focusing just on numbers. The alternative to "mass incarceration" cannot be "normal incarceration." While we can fight for the immediate reduction of the prison population, we do not want the same type of prison system on a smaller scale.

Challenging the character, not just the scale, of the criminal injustice system requires identifying what we aim to change and what should replace it. In this concluding chapter, we examine several of the reform proposals coming from ruling-class circles and then propose another vision worth fighting for.

RIGHT-WING POLICY PROPOSALS

Those right-wing architects of mass incarceration, currently masquerading as its critics, have no real solution. ALEC has put together a draft bill called the "Conditional Early-Release Bond," which proposes that correctional authorities release inmates early with a bond guaranteed by a "surety" (insurer). Theoretically, a bail bondsman could offer this service, but in many states this would likely serve as a boost for the corporate insurance industry.

Once released, under this right-wing plan, an inmate's freedom would be contingent on meeting a number of conditions set by the state. ALEC recommends the former inmate must hold a job, take drug tests, meet various reporting requirements, pay restitution or court costs, be subject to GPS monitoring, and/or participate in specified community service, among other things. The insurer would only be liable for payment if the "principal" (the ex-inmate) were not returned to custody 180 days after a breach of the terms of release. The insurer ("surety") would also have the ability to arrest the "principal" in the result of a breach.

It is clear what this is: The ALEC bill simply replaces mass incarceration with an expanded and privatized system of parole. It would require inmates and their families to pay an insurance company for the right to remain free. Further, it would create a layer of militarized "collection agents" that would be responsible for rounding up those who had violated the terms of their release. Just as bail bondsmen employ bounty hunters, insurers would inevitably have to employ their own staff of glorified bounty hunters to maintain control over the insured persons.

How far such ALEC bills will go is still unclear, but its inclusion of rehabilitation, job and community services could potentially win support from Democratic politicians who want to present themselves as proactive on the issues of crime and mass incarceration. The key to this legislation is privatization, whether it comes with more lenient or strict terms of release. It presents a way to reduce the prison population (and thus state costs) while creating new expenses for released inmates and a boom for private correctional and insurance businesses. The American Probation and Parole Association put it plainly over a decade ago: Such bills are "motivated by financial profit."[1] Apparently unsatisfied with making profits on the inmate's initial incarceration, phone calls and cheap labor, the private correctional industry hopes to even score big from his or her release!

ALEC offers another bill called the "Recidivism Reduction Act," which would have states implement "evidence-based" best practices to reduce re-offending. Such unobjectionable-sounding bills may give ALEC the appearance of a politically neutral institution to some progressives. In fact, the lobbying group is comprised of a number of corporations, focused on crafting "free-market" strategies for both conservative and liberal politicians. Given that this is the same coalition that crafted mass incarceration to begin with, we cannot afford to be fooled by such "reformers."

CONVERTING SOCIETY INTO A PRISON

Heather Mac Donald of the Manhattan Institute, a conservative political commentator and defender of harsh law-and-order policies, has another answer to mass incarceration: more police. Mac Donald has approvingly cited the performance of the NYPD over the last two decades, saying that its aggressive policing has been an effective deterrent to mass incarceration. (You can't make this stuff up!)

Mac Donald points to the declines in crime in New York City, which has outpaced the national average. Mac Donald argues that while misdemeanor arrests and convictions rose in New York City, felony arrests and convictions fell. As with the "broken windows" idea, she argues that increased policing of less serious crimes, and putting youth in Rikers Island for short stays, sends "the message to potential criminals that the police are watching."[2] While poor Black and Latino neighborhoods have faced constant harassment and brutality, Mac Donald celebrates this as the "greatest public policy success" of the last 25 years. Rejecting the notion that the police are an instrument of racism, she says they merely operate in the highest-crime neighborhoods. Mac Donald's paternalism reaches its peak when she claims that, because of heavy policing, "more than 10,000 black and Hispanic males are alive today who would have been killed had homicide rates remained at the levels of the early 1990s."[3]

Mac Donald also notes the close connection between the massive show of police force and gentrification, as "cutting-edge restaurants opened in what used to be forlorn drug outposts."

PHOTO: KHAMPHA BOUAPHANH

*More cops, more arrests and more prisoners typically
accompany efforts to gentrify urban communities.*

This is a crucial observation to our analysis of mass incarceration: It corresponded with the capitalist reclaiming of urban space for redevelopment. "Post-industrial" service-sector and finance-oriented cities required large influxes of new (mostly white) more affluent residents, businesses and students. The re-urbanization of these strata of the population, which a generation earlier had migrated to the suburbs, depended on upending the perception of the city as a den of criminal activity.[4] This "urban renewal" agenda, typically propagated through racist imagery, meant more cops, more arrests and more prisoners in the most oppressed communities. "Clean up the city" did not mean cleaning up hospitals, schools, libraries and housing in such areas; it meant cleansing the city of the "problem elements."

What Mac Donald proposes is to release more poor and working people from prison to then supervise them more closely in their communities. She calls for the intensification of the policing and gentrification regime, alongside intensified surveillance technologies. This is not tearing down the prison walls, but moving them geographically—ending mass incarceration by converting entire neighborhoods to unofficial open-air prisons.

Such proposals could gain traction among a section of political elites and even some misguided activists. Combined together, they provide the skeleton of a long-range capitalist reform plan for mass incarceration without forsaking the "fight against crime." In the short term, the number of individuals in prison could be significantly reduced, and supervised by private business. In appearance, this would give nonviolent drug offenders the chance to get out and restart their lives, and potentially enter treatment and job programs. It would produce an extensive monitoring system to discourage ex-inmates' supposed "propensities" to commit crime. It could reduce budgets.

At the same time, such a reform package would assuage fears about releasing prisoners by promoting a "surge" of highly equipped and armed police to patrol high-crime areas and "shake the confidence" of criminals. In addition, they promise that more police would reduce crime and deter at-risk youth from the path towards the dangerous underworld. In this rosy—but utterly false—picture, the necessary inconvenience of masses of police in the short term would in the long term translate into an improved quality of life. As time goes on, they claim, social behaviors and attitudes would be changed, and mass incarceration policies would become less necessary.

Everything about this vision is wrong.

RETHINKING CRIME, RETHINKING THE SYSTEM

What's not to like with the above "reforms" to mass incarceration? Quite a bit. First off, the vision of reform as presented above leaves out the crucial issue of how society defines crime. As we have mentioned before, the meaning of crime is based on the shifting boundaries of the law and the "ruling ideas" of a given society at a given time. Let us look at the "war on drugs," which has driven mass incarceration. Many have pointed out the deleterious effects of alcohol use, or addictive prescription drugs, but these are legal. Alcohol causes more deaths and social dysfunction than marijuana, yet it is both legal and socially acceptable to drink copious amounts of alcohol in a variety of settings. Why is marijuana stigmatized and criminalized, responsible for huge numbers of arrests, violations, fines and prisoners? There is no good answer that would not also implicate alcohol or tobacco.

It is impossible to talk about mass incarceration without undoing the pointless and destructive "war on drugs." Some have pointed to decriminalization of drugs as the answer.

For sure, bringing the illegal drug industry into the formal capitalist economy would have certain benefits. It would mean the regulation of contracts, quality, certain aspects of customer service, and labor rules. One could theoretically sue for payment, or a boss who mistreats workers, and market competition could be regulated. In the underground economy, without official rules, force reigns supreme. If someone fails to pay up, they are beaten or killed. In the underground economy, one's share of the market is protected by pure force. A "hostile takeover," a regular occurrence in the corporate world, takes on far bloodier implications, as one must be able to physically defeat the competition. To rise through the ranks of an underground economic unit, one often has to engage in violent behavior.

In other words, the routine and devastating violence associated with the drug industry—a stimulus for mass incarceration—can largely be attributed to its existence outside the boundaries of legally codified rules. This pattern is apparent throughout the history of capitalism. The same was true of the European colonial enterprises as they scrambled to control trans-Atlantic slavery and commerce; what began as violent piracy ended up regulated as matters of diplomacy (still punctuated by periodic competitive wars, of course). The same was true of the free-for-all land-grabbing that was the material base of the genocidal and inter-settler violence of the "Wild West." Most famously, the prohibition of alcohol directly stimulated the rise of violent crime syndicates—a "lumpen bourgeoisie" operating outside the law. Sociopathic behavior, although undoubtedly fostered in such conditions, was not the root cause of the violence in each of these examples.

Clearly there is a history of obscenely brutal forms of accumulation that exist outside the formal economy becoming integrated into "respectable" business. But isolated demands to decriminalize or legalize drugs, as proposed by libertarians who want to respect an individual's "choice" to use drugs, are insufficient. They merely become avenues for corporate enrichment at the expense of oppressed communities—corporations that will then have a material incentive, and large advertising apparatus—aimed at encouraging addiction.

Drug use and addiction are destructive public health epidemics. The Black Panther Party famously issued a pamphlet called "Capitalism + Dope = Genocide." Operating in a context in which the Black liberation movement was electrifying and educating thousands of youth, the BPP exposed and combated drug syndicates as accomplices of the state, peddling self-destruction and passivity. Likewise, a movement to end mass incarceration today cannot simply be a movement for the state to leave drug-infested communities alone. It must be linked to a broader transformative project over for whom government works, how society's resources are utilized, and ultimately who holds power.

Former addicts universally attest that curing addiction depends on changing the life circumstances that led to the addiction in the first place. Thus, an effort to defeat the drug epidemic cannot be confined to medical treatment; it requires treating the social conditions that give rise to hopelessness and escapism on a mass scale.

Some liberal opponents of mass incarceration draw a sharp distinction between violent and non-violent criminals, arguing that only the latter should be released. But the above demonstrates how violence itself must be situated in a specific social and economic context. This does not excuse reprehensible violent crimes against the community, but shows that in a different socioeconomic context—when resources are liberated and the oppressed come to control the criminal justice system—there would be much greater room for individual redemption and participation in society. History has proven that so-called "career criminals" can become not only productive members of society, but powerful leaders. Malcolm X, George Jackson and Tookie Williams are case studies, transforming themselves and those around them after connecting to a movement for a higher social objective.

What are the conditions under which we can effect a similar transformation of those who have transgressed against the people? The concept of redemption—although typically associated with religion—has a role to play in a non-religious movement against mass incarceration. There is no avoiding the fact that in a more lenient criminal justice system, in which people are freed from prison or not incarcerated at all, some will return to destructive behavior towards themselves and others. But we must challenge the "zero tolerance" worldview, which slaps the label of "criminal" on individuals to justify their permanent removal or subordination in society. We must challenge the demands for ever more state surveillance—as if safety in one's community can only be achieved with the threat of repression and at the expense of our collective civil liberties. Instead of a type of society that accepts punishment and incarceration for widespread crimes, we can insist on one that is truly rehabilitative and comprehensive. In the process of fighting mass incarceration policies, there is an opportunity to do precisely that—to assert not only that the roots of crime must be attacked, but that those currently in prison can be productive members of society.

> We must challenge the demands for ever more state surveillance—as if safety in one's community can only be achieved with the threat of repression and at the expense of our collective civil liberties.

If framed this way, the debate is not over who to let out of prison, but how we challenge the bourgeois view of "crime." How can the social roots of distinct crimes be addressed, and what sort of society will give individuals a second and third chance?

This discussion of an alternative system need not devolve into idle chatter or utopianism, where we merely draw up an ideal society. The Party for Socialism and Liberation starts with the two premises that 1) poor and working people have the capacity to lead, and 2) the wealth exists to rapidly transform the social and economic conditions for the masses of people. Every person can be provided a meaningful income, as well as guaranteed housing, educational opportunities, child care and health care (including mental health). It is possible to have political structures and institutions that empower, rather than disenfranchise and limit the masses of people. Suffice it to say that the capitalist class is unwilling and unable to carry out such transformations. To achieve this sort of government requires a different social structure, and therefore a revolution.

The remaking of the educational system, as well as popular culture, would promote a different set of values. Instead of an army of officers who specialize in harassment and brutality, a government of poor and working people could deploy an army of formerly incarcerated peace-keepers to address the lingering legacies of gang culture.

This is just the tip of the iceberg; once the resources of society have been liberated from Wall Street, the possibilities are endless.

We must fight for additional job programs and drug treatment centers in the here and now, but we need more. As this account has demonstrated, mass incarceration has been caused by U.S. capitalist economic development, capitalist values and the conscious strategies of capitalist policymakers. There is no getting around the reality of modern capitalism, in which whole communities have essentially been left to rot, while wages and benefits are declining and job opportunities are subject to the desired profit margins and stock dividends of Wall Street. Those on the losing side of this dynamic, who experience all the attendant social problems, have been steadily corralled into the prison system.

It may be possible to reduce the scale of incarceration with adjustments to the criminal justice system, but this will do nothing to treat the underlying social relation of crime. It may be possible to legalize certain drugs, but this will do little to address the economic and health crises in our communities. If we limit our conversation strictly to numbers of inmates, narrow drug decriminalization efforts, or certain categories of prisoners, we do a disservice to the broader transformation that is needed.

The problem is not just that the government spends too much money on prisons or puts too many people in jail. It is that the current system thrives on poverty, unemployment, national oppression, racism, militarism and stark inequality—crimes in and of themselves—while imprisoning the victims of these phenomena. Fighting mass incarceration, therefore, must call into question the sort of society we have now and what we want it to be. We cannot "solve" crime without solving the social question. That is the position of revolutionaries, such as the workers and activists who are members of the Party for Socialism and Liberation—join us! □

Appendices

Free all
political prisoners

THERE are those who believe there are no real "political prisoners" in America. In fact, there are at least 100 political prisoners held inside prison cells across this country. As we have described in this book, the U.S. government waged a vicious war on radical organizations during the 1960s and 1970s. While not exclusively from this era, most political prisoners currently locked away are there because of their long histories of revolutionary activism. Some are held because of bold actions they took in furtherance of revolutionary goals; others are there on clear frame-ups, traps set to neutralize their leadership of movements of revolutionary-minded people.

While branded as criminals, these individuals are truly comrades in the struggle of all those opposed to the U.S. capitalist-imperialist system. It is important to note that whether we approve or not of any particular alleged action of any particular individual, we do not consider them to be "crimes." Rather, even actions we do not endorse fall under the "higher law" of a people's right to resist oppression and exploitation, and make revolutionary change.

While the list of political prisoners is unfortunately long, we choose to highlight a selection of individuals here as a tribute to their contributions to the broader revolutionary movement.

We have provided websites at the end of each entry where you can get more information on the case, and where to write to the prisoners. In addition to those listed, we urge everyone to support all political prisoners, including some of the following who can be contacted via the information on the following page.

Free all political prisoners now! □

Jalil Muntaqim
Jalil Muntaqim/A. Bottom
#77A4283
Attica C.F.
P.O. Box 149
Attica, NY 14011-0149
www.freejalil.com/

Sekou Odinga
#09A3775
Clinton C.F.
P.O. Box 2001
Dannemora, NY 12929
www.sekouodinga.com/about.html

Marshall E. Conway
#116469
Jessup Correctional Institute
P.O. Box 534
Jessup, MD 20794
http://www.freeeddieconway.org/

Russell Maroon Shoatz
#AF-3855
301 Morea Road
Frackville, PA 17932
http://russellmaroonshoats.wordpress.com/about/

Mumia Abu-Jamal

PHOTO: PRISON RADIO

IN his days as a radio disc jockey, Mumia Abu-Jamal became known as the "voice of the voiceless," an apt moniker accurately describing his continued advocacy on behalf of all exploited and oppressed people. His is one of the most prominent faces among political prisoners held in America.

Born Wesley Cook in 1954, Mumia, a native of Philadelphia, took the name Mumia Abu-Jamal after a Kenyan teacher gave him the Swahili name in class. Mumia cut his political teeth as a member of the Black Panther Party in his hometown of Philadelphia and also served with the Panthers across the country in both Oakland and New York City.

Joining at the age of 15, Mumia quickly became a young leader in the Panthers. He began writing for the Black Panther newspaper, later strategizing in the case of the Panther 21 in New York City, and being one of the party leaders sent to Chicago in the wake of the murder of Fred Hampton.

After the decline and destruction of the BPP, Mumia returned to Philadelphia, where he became a renowned journalist, where he first earned his reputation as the "voice of the voiceless." Mumia exposed all sorts of abuses in Philadelphia, including the crimes of the brutal, racist Philadelphia police department. His courageous journalism led to his 1980 election as president of the Philadelphia Association of Black Journalists.

Mumia also became a member of the MOVE organization, a Black commune based primarily in Philadelphia. It was the target of heavy police repression, eventually including the dropping of a bomb on their headquarters in 1985 by Philadelphia police and federal authorities.

In 1981, Mumia was close to the scene of the murder of Police Officer Daniel Faulkner. Faulkner was killed and Mumia was framed for his murder. Mumia's initial trial was essentially a kangaroo court where the prosecution and a racist judge schemed to execute Mumia, using his radical activities in a base attempt to smear him.

The judge—Albert Sabo—at one time held the record for sending the most people to death row, and also had record numbers of cases reversed on appeal, something that aptly gave him the reputation as a "hanging judge." A court reporter even overheard him remark about Mumia's trial, "I'm going to help them fry the n*****."

Further, the jury was picked in such a way to favor white Philadelphians who the prosecution felt, correctly in this case, were much more likely to be swayed by their anti-radical, racist arguments. It has also come to light since the trial that bribing and coercion of witnesses as well as false testimony were used in Mumia's initial trial, which resulted in a death sentence.

Mumia has now been locked away in the U.S. prison system for more than 30 years, most of that time held on death row in solitary confinement. While he has recently been released from solitary with a commuted death sentence, this has only been the result of vigorous struggle on his behalf. While Mumia no longer faces the death penalty, the U.S. government and State of Pennsylvania are determined to keep him locked up for the rest of his life.

It deserves mention, however, that Mumia remains unbowed. His case has become a rallying cry for millions across the world, and he has written six books and countless articles that are read widely. His recorded commentaries are a mainstay at progressive political events across the country, where his voice is greeted with cheers. If it has been said once, it should be said a million times: Free Mumia now! ☐

http://freemumia.com

Dr. Mutulu Shakur

DR. Mutulu Shakur, father of late hip-hop great Tupac Shakur, whether in the streets or behind bars has been one of the most stalwart examples revolutionary dedication. Born in Baltimore, Md., in 1950, Shakur was raised from the age of seven in the Jamaica neighborhood of Queens, New York. Becoming politically active at the age of 16, he was a member of the Revolutionary Action Movement as well as a close collaborator of the Black Panther Party, of which his brother Lumumba was a member. Shakur was also associated with the Provisional Government of the Republic of New Afrika. an organization dedicated to setting up an independent Black state in the southern United States. Shakur became an active member and director of political education of the Lincoln Detox Community Program at Lincoln Hospital in the South Bronx in 1970. The Lincoln Program was an outgrowth of the demands from the surrounding neighborhood for a drug detoxification clinic at the local hospital. The doctor was among a number of radical activists who helped run and shape the program, which became one of the first to use acupuncture as a method of detoxification.

Licensed to practice acupuncture in 1976, Shakur eventually became assistant director of the program, which became one of the most successful drug rehabilitation centers. He went on to found the Harlem Institute of Acupuncture and the Black Acupuncture Advisory Association of North America in 1978, where he continued his practice, toured the world speaking on his methods, and trained hundreds in acupuncture techniques. This followed continued activism in a number of arenas including as a member of the Charles Cobb Commission for Racial Justice for the National Council of Churches.

In 1982, Shakur was charged in a conspiracy trial with a number of others, accused as both a conspirator and mastermind of an armed revolutionary group that had carried out a number of operations, and as the mastermind behind the escape of jailed revolutionary Assata Shakur. Arrested in 1986 after time spent underground, he was sentenced to 60 years with no parole.

First and foremost, the very idea of trying Shakur and any of his alleged co-conspirators under the Racketeer Influenced and Corrupt Organizations Act, designed to assist in prosecuting organized crime, is an outrage. Revolutionary activity of any sort is certainly not "racketeering" nor is it a "corrupt" act. It is not a question of endorsing any particular activity but one of basic principle—attempting to make a revolution is not a crime!

Like the cases of most political prisoners, Shakur's trial was more show than substance, where snitch testimony was a significant feature. One informant for the government was rewarded with $110,000 in material benefits plus a reduced sentence! Even the trial judge admitted that the doctor had been the victim of illegal government surveillance and harassment under the COINTEL program. Other than the one paid snitch, the prosecution had no physical evidence linking Shakur to any of the alleged crime scenes, and no eyewitness testimony to his presence.

All appeals have been denied by the courts, and while a sentence reduction is possible, it is clear that the authorities are determined to keep Shakur locked behind bars for the rest of his natural life. However, he has never been silenced and continues to agitate on behalf of political prisoners and oppressed people everywhere. Dr. Mutulu Shakur is a revolutionary, not a criminal. Free him now! ☐

http://mutulushakur.com/site/case-facts/

Leonard Peltier

THE continued imprisonment of Leonard Peltier is a signal example of the desire of the U.S. imperialist government to keep Native nations subjugated, and prevent any recognition of their sovereignty. Born in the mid-1940s in North Dakota, Peltier was raised on both the Turtle Mountain Chippewa and Fort Totten Sioux reservations. Hailing from the Anishinabe, Dakota and Lakota nations, he locates his own political consciousness and will to struggle in the brutal, racist, impoverished existence for Natives of most reservations.

While politically active from the age of 14, his first major political act was participation in the takeover of Fort Lawton in Seattle in 1970. Despite Native Americans having clear rights to the abandoned base, and being entirely peaceable, they were brutally evicted by the U.S. government. Despite this initial setback, however, Fort Lawton was eventually converted into a Native American cultural center. Shortly after this, Peltier moved to Colorado where he became a member of the American Indian Movement, a nationwide organization fighting for the rights of Native people, which was a part and parcel of the radical upsurge of oppressed communities during the late 1960s and early 1970s.

As part of AIM, he took part in the 1972 Trail of Broken Treaties March on Washington, D.C., which resulted in a bold sit-in where Native activists occupied the Bureau of Indian Affairs building. Shortly after, Peltier was framed for the murder of a Milwaukee police officer, causing him to go underground. Despite being a fugitive from the (in)justice system, Peltier traveled widely across the country assisting in the struggles of Native peoples, often in a security capacity. He also participated in efforts to revive traditional native practices, particularly on the Pine Ridge reservation in South Dakota.

In 1975, Peltier was arrested for the killing of two FBI agents on the Pine Ridge reservation, in what was a clear frame-up to remove him from active struggle in the Native people's movement. The agents were killed during a time of an increasing political struggle between the so-called tribal leadership allied with the government on one side and AIM on the other. The FBI and the aptly named GOON squad of tribal police had carried out serious harassment and attacks on AIM members and supporters. The two agents were involved in a shootout that ultimately involved 40 AIM members and 150 FBI, BIA and GOON forces.

Despite the fact that there were allegedly 40 AIM members involved, the government only indicted three central AIM leaders for the killing of the two officers. Peltier, fearing he could not receive a fair trial, fled to Canada. The government used the coerced and false testimony of a woman alleging to have witnessed the incident to have him extradited.

The other two AIM leaders charged were acquitted as a jury had found their actions justifiable given the significant atmosphere of terror against AIM on Pine Ridge. To prevent a similar outcome in Peltier's trial, large amounts of evidence from the situation at Pine Ridge, conflicting ballistics reports and evidence of FBI misconduct were all excluded. Peltier was sentenced to two life terms and continues to be imprisoned today. It would be a mistake, however, to think that Peltier's efforts had been stopped by placing him behind bars. He has remained a strong voice for Native peoples, using his own plight to elevate knowledge of that struggle, in addition to showing solidarity with movements of the oppressed around the world.

He also has been an active humanitarian, helping to organize scholarships for Native law students, toy drives for children at Pine Ridge, and even an art benefit for the victims of the 2010 Haitian earthquake. We in the Party for Socialism and Liberation are also proud to say that Peltier was gracious enough to send our 2010 National Conference a message of support that was received with a standing ovation by hundreds of attendees. Leonard Peltier must go free now! □

http://www.whoisleonardpeltier.info/

Sundiata Acoli

BORN in 1939 as Clark Edward Squire, Sundiata Acoli was raised in Vernon, Texas. He attended Prairie-View A&M University, a historically Black college, graduating in 1956 with a Bachelor of Arts in mathematics. Over the next 13 years, Acoli would use his expertise to work in the computer industry across the New York area. Swept

up with millions of others into the movements of the 1960s, Acoli was present during the 1964 Freedom Summer, and engaged in voter registration drives in Mississippi.

In 1968, Acoli joined the Harlem section of the Black Panther Party, becoming an active participant in the whole range of the party's activities. He was one of the party members arrested in 1969 as part of what would become known as the Panther 21 case. Held on $100,000 bail, the Panther 21 were slapped with bogus charges of conspiring to bomb a number of locations in New York City, including the Botanical Gardens, several department stores and a police station.

After a two-year trial that sparked mass protests around the country, the Panther 21 were acquitted of all charges—the jury brought back the verdict in less than two hours. Acoli continued his revolutionary activism following the trial, and continued to be a target for police repression. In 1973, Acoli, Assata Shakur and Zayd Shakur were ambushed on the New Jersey Turnpike by state troopers, who killed Zayd and wounded Assata. One trooper died and another was wounded in the shootout. Despite the gun that killed the trooper was found near the body of someone other than Acoli, he was (along with Assata) charged with that murder and convicted after something less than a fair trial. Acoli was placed in a supermax-style cell created just for him, where for five years he was let out only 10 minutes a day for a shower and two hours twice a week for recreation. Acoli was sent to the federal prison located in Marion, Ill., one of the pioneers of the supermax concept, where he was locked down 23 hours a day. Acoli continues to be locked away on a life plus 30 years sentence, with parole denied predicated on his unwillingness to admit that his dedication to revolutionary ideals was a mistake. As such, authorities do not find him to be suitably "rehabilitated." Nevertheless, Acoli has remained one of the most active voices from inside the prison system on the rights of prisoners and the cause of revolutionary struggle. Not one more day! Free Sundiata Acoli now! □

http://www.sundiataacoli.org/about

Assata Shakur

ON May 2, 2013, the Federal Bureau of Investigation announced that they had placed Assata Shakur on its "Most Wanted Terrorists" list, making her the first woman to be so designated. The state of New Jersey also raised the bounty on her head to $2 million. These government actions came on the 40th anniversary of the shootout in which police allege that Shakur killed an officer.

Shakur has been living in exile in Cuba for the last 29 years. Her real crime, FBI spokesman Aaron Ford said, was that from Cuba she continues to "maintain and promote her ... ideology" and "provides anti-U.S. government speeches espousing the Black Liberation Army message"—an ideology and message that the U.S. government has declared "terrorism."

Assata Shakur was born JoAnne Chesimard, and her name change reflected her desire to identify with the revolutionary struggles of her African heritage. Assata means "she who struggles." Her middle name, Olugbala, means "love for the people." Shakur was a name taken in honor of her comrade Zayd Shakur.

Assata was active in the Black liberation movement, the student rights movement, and the movement to end the war in Vietnam. She joined the Black Panther Party, which became the target of the FBI's infamous COINTELPRO effort to destroy it and its leaders.

Shakur was falsely convicted of having killed a police officer on May 2, 1973. While driving on the New Jersey Turnpike, Assata, Zayd Shakur and Sundiata Acoli were stopped by state troopers, allegedly for having a "faulty taillight." A shootout ensued where one state trooper killed Zayd Shakur, and another trooper, Werner Foerster, ended up dead. Assata Shakur was charged with both murders, despite the fact that the other trooper, James Harper, admitted he killed Zayd Shakur.

Assata had been following police instructions, standing with her hands in the air, when she was shot twice by Harper, including a bullet to the back. Tests done by the police found that Shakur had not fired a gun, and no physical or medical evidence was presented by the prosecution to back up their claim that she had fired a gun at Trooper Harper.

While in trial proceedings, the state attempted to pin six other serious crimes on her, alleging she had carried out bank robberies, kidnappings and attempted killings. She was acquitted three times, two charges were dismissed and one resulted in a hung jury.

Shakur was put on trial in a county where due to pre-trial publicity 70 percent of people thought she was guilty. She was judged by an all-white jury. Without any physical evidence to present, the prosecution relied on false statements and innuendo aimed at playing on the prejudices of the jury pool against Black people, political radicals, and Black revolutionaries in particular. Finally, after years behind bars, the state secured her conviction for the turnpike shooting.

After more than six years incarcerated under brutal conditions, Shakur escaped from the maximum security wing of the Clinton Correctional Facility for Women in New Jersey in 1979 and later moved to Cuba. She continues to advocate for revolutionary change to this day.

Placing Shakur on the "Most Wanted Terrorists" list is also an attack on Cuba. On May 1, 2013, the United States refused to remove Cuba from the "State Sponsors of Terrorism" list. The next day, Shakur became a "Most Wanted Terrorist." By claiming that Cuba supports "terrorism" and is harboring a "terrorist," the U.S. government provides itself with a pretext to continue the illegal blockade of Cuba and starve the revolution of trade.

Because Shakur remains a symbol of resistance and is unrepentant in her politics, the government will never stop their attempts to smear, kidnap or kill her. But millions of people know the truth. Her legacy cannot be whitewashed or dismissed. Even though she is in Cuba, the government remains afraid of her example. They know that while decades have passed, the conditions still exist to give birth to a million Assata Shakurs. ☐

http://www.assatashakur.org/

Puerto Rican Political Prisoners

OSCAR López Rivera, Avelino González Claudio, and Norberto González Claudio are three Puerto Rican freedom fighters imprisoned by the U.S. government as part of its campaign to keep Puerto Rico locked in colonial status. Puerto Rico has been colonized by Spain and then the United States for 500 years. Following the Spanish-American War, without consultation of any kind, the United States seized control of Puerto Rico as a term of their peace agreement with Spain. The United States installed a U.S. governor and declared martial law.

Since then, the United States has continued its occupation of Puerto Rico, never giving its people a true opportunity to weigh in on independence. Even the right-wing pro-statehood Puerto Ricans cynically use the term self-determination to describe their position, further evidence that Puerto Rico is an oppressed nation.

Over the years of domination true freedom fighters struggling for Puerto Rico's independence from colonial powers have emerged, often in the guise of armed underground organizations. The Puerto Rican political prisoners have been proud members of this movement for independence and engaged in a range of actions in defense of their people's sovereignty. The U.S. government calls this terrorism. People of conscience call it heroism.

Oscar López Rivera was born in San Sebastián, Puerto Rico, in 1943. Moving to Chicago when he was 12, Rivera later became an active member of progressive movements in the Puerto Rican community and helped contribute to a number of crucial projects, including being among the founders of what is now known as Dr. Pedro Albizu Campos High School in Chicago. He was arrested in 1981 after five years underground, and has been imprisoned ever since. He rejected an offer of leniency in 1999, unwilling to accept parole, although he maintains total solidarity with other Puerto Rican freedom fighters who took conditional clemency offered by the government.

Avelino González Claudio was accused in 1985 of participating in a $7 million expropriation of Wells Fargo by Puerto Rican independence organization Los Macheteros. Not arrested at the time, Avelino was picked up in 2008 and sentenced to seven years for his alleged role in the operation. Born in 1942 in Vega Baja, Puerto Rico, Avelino is a longtime activist in the Puerto Rican independence movement in both New York and Puerto Rico, including administering the journal Pensamiento Critico.

Norberto Gonzáles Claudio, also born in Vega Baja, has been a member of the independence movement since the 1960s. He was active in student and workers' struggles, participating in the garbage collectors strike of 1970, and the 1970 and 1971 student strikes at the University of Puerto Rico, as well as participating in protests against mining in Adjuntas.

These three men are examples of the steadfastness of the Puerto Rican independence struggle. Dedication to ending U.S. colonialism is no crime! Free the Puerto Rican political prisoners! Independence for Puerto Rico! □

http://www.prolibertadweb.com/index.html

Angola 3

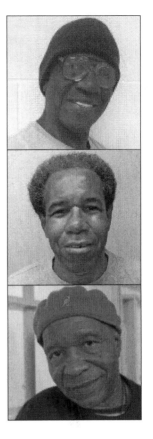

HERMAN Wallace, Albert Woodfox and Robert King were charged with murders they did not commit for their part in fighting segregation inside Louisiana's plantation prison system. While not politically active upon arriving in prison, the brutal conditions inside and a raging Black freedom movement on the outside prompted the Angola 3 to form a Black Panther Party chapter behind bars.

Wallace, Woodfox, King and others routinely spoke and acted out against injustice. Using hunger and work strikes, the Angola 3 forced the attention of Louisiana's notoriously corrupt politicians and local media in the early 1970s. The militants called for investigations into a host of unconstitutional and extraordinarily inhumane practices commonplace in what was then the "bloodiest prison in the South." Eager to put an end to outside scrutiny, prison officials began punishing inmates they saw as troublemakers.

At the height of this institutional chaos, Wallace, Woodfox and King were charged with murders they did not commit and thrown into tiny solitary-confinement cells. King was released in 2001, but Wallace and Woodfox remain in solitary, continuing to fight for their freedom. At 71 years of age, Wallace faces terminal cancer, and an international campaign is underway to win his compassionate release.

In 1972, a young white guard named Brent Miller was fatally stabbed in Angola Prison. Wallace and Woodfox were immediately assumed to be guilty, thrown into solitary without an investigation, and eventually convicted of the crime. King was not in Angola at the time but accused of being a distant conspirator. He was later charged and convicted of the murder of another prisoner.

During the decades of their appeals, DNA evidence was "lost," the state's main witness was bribed by officials with cigarettes and favorable conditions, and today even the guard's widow doubts their guilt and calls their trials unfair. A bloody fingerprint at the scene does not match either Wallace or Woodfox, and no attempt was ever made to match it with another prisoner. Both men had alibi witnesses with nothing to gain by testifying that they were far from the scene when the stabbing occurred.

In 2001, King was released after proving his innocence, but the appeals of Wallace and Woodfox have stalled, despite new evidence of their innocence. To this day, they remain defiant. Angola's current warden, Burl Cain, says: "The thing about [Woodfox] is that he wants to demonstrate. He wants to organize. There is no such thing as a peaceful demonstration in prison."

Free Albert Woodfox and Herman Wallace now!

http://www.angola3.org

MOVE 9

MEMBERS of the MOVE organization have been the target of some of the most vicious state repression meted out to domestic opponents of the government, having been repeatedly beaten, shot at and ultimately bombed. The MOVE 9 are members of the MOVE organization falsely imprisoned in 1978 for the murder of police officer James Ramp in Philadelphia.

MOVE, formed in the early 1970s by John Africa, was a Black commune organized around the concept of preservation of human, plant and animal life. The primary MOVE house was in Philadelphia, whose mayor and former police chief, Frank Rizzo, tolerated no forms of dissent and brutally repressed progressive movements, on top of ruling over the so-called ghetto with his corrupt and ultra-violent police force. Rizzo was an unabashed and open racist, expressing clear contempt for Black people, radicals, the LGBT community, and basically anyone not a part of his white "ethnic" coalition.

In the mid-1970s, three MOVE women suffered miscarriages due to police beatings. In 1976, a baby's skull was crushed by rampaging police officers beating MOVE members during a raid, something denied by police but revealed by journalist Mumia Abu-Jamal.

MOVE continued to enrage the Philadelphia police by refusing to give in, and holding public rallies to state their defiance to Rizzo and his cops. Rizzo escalated the struggle, sealing off a four-block radius around the MOVE house and refusing to let anything, including food, through in an attempt to starve out the MOVE organization. When political pressure against such an egregious tactic forced them to end the two-month blockade, the "authorities" set a 90-day deadline for MOVE to leave their home.

When this arbitrary deadline passed, the capitalist courts signed a number of arrest warrants for MOVE members. On Aug. 8, 1978, the Philadelphia police moved in with bulldozers, cranes and hundreds of officers. Upon finding MOVE barricaded in their basement, they used high-pressure hoses in an attempt to flood them out. At this point, gunshots came from somewhere, most likely from across the street. Philadelphia police unleashed a fusillade of bullets—over 2,000—at the MOVE house. In the gunfire, police officer James Ramp was killed. After surrendering, the MOVE members were brutalized, with Delbert Africa's beating at the hands of police covered on live television.

The ensuing trial of MOVE members was typical of the kangaroo courts that followed frame-up operations of the Philadelphia police in those days. The crime scene was bulldozed, evidence was manipulated, and the judge was hostile to MOVE. In the spring of 1980, Janine, Debbie, Janet, Merle, Delbert, Mike, Phil, Eddie and Chuck Africa were given 30-100 years on charges related to the death of Officer Ramp, including third-degree murder.

To this day, the nine remain locked away, denied parole, despite clearly being victims of a vendetta on the part of the Philadelphia police and Mayor Frank Rizzo. Forty years is too long! Free the MOVE 9 now! □

http://www.move9parole.blogspot.com/

The Cuban Five

THE case of the Cuban Five, unlike the other political prisoners profiled here, is not a result of the suppression of radical movements that birthed the "law and order" ideology. Their transgression is to have been affiliated with a revolutionary government the American ruling class is opposed to. Their case is an example of how the mass incarceration machine, built as a method of social control, can be deployed against more than just "domestic" political opponents.

The Cuban Five were railroaded into prison for defending the Cuban people from U.S.-sponsored terrorism that has cost the lives of over 3,400 Cubans. Gerardo Hernández, Ramón Labañino, Antonio Guerrero, Fernando González and René González were deeply influenced by the ideals of the Cuban Revolution as they grew up. Three of them—Gerardo, René and Fernando—volunteered with the Cuban military mission in Angola to defend that country against the South African apartheid regime

When CIA-backed Cuban-exile terrorist organizations began to increase their plots against Cuba in the early 1990s, the Cuban Five volunteered to thwart the terrorist plans. They never possessed any weapons. They were arrested on Sept. 12, 1998, on 26 federal counts, falsely charged with espionage conspiracy and held in solitary confinement for 17 months in Miami, known as the heartland of the exile-terrorist groups, before their trial began in November 2000.

A witch-hunt atmosphere prevailed before and during their trial. Yet the federal judge denied defense motions to move the venue out of Miami. Important evidence has emerged proving the U.S. government made secret payments to dozens of Miami reporters at the time of the Five's trial, constituting corruption of justice. The Cuban Five were convicted June 8, 2001, and sentenced to a total of four life terms and 75 years in December 2001.

On Aug. 9, 2005, the Cuban Five won an unprecedented victory on appeal. However, the Bush administration appealed, and the full panel of the 11th Circuit Court affirmed their convictions. Later court decisions reduced the sentences of three of the Five. René González was released on Oct. 7, 2011, and after 18 months of probation, returned to a hero's welcome in Cuba. Free the Five Now! □

www.freethefive.org

A letter from prison

This letter was written by a prisoner in California's Pelican Bay Prison Secure Housing Unit (SHU) to Ben Becker, editor of Liberation, *the newspaper of the Party for Socialism and Liberation. It is included here as a valuable contribution on the issue of mass incaceration.*

February 21, 2013
Brother Ben,

Your letter dated 2-14-13 was well received. I hope that you all are pushing onward in the aftermath of "Hurricane Sandy" as well. I was glad you all enjoyed my letter and art and that in revolutionary spirit I was there with you all as well. You all are here with me as well as I use the centerfold posters in *Liberation* to cover my walls in my cell, so I am always comforted with the excellent posters of resistance!

Your book project sounds wonderful, Michelle Alexander's book "The New Jim Crow" was a good start but it negated the political aspect of our oppression, this of course must be covered in a revolutionary analysis of Amerikan prisons, as well as giving the people a roadmap out of the oppression—which "The New Jim Crow" did not do. Your book is much needed especially in this juncture and the budding anti-imperialist prison movement that is developing. I hope to use this book in my work here and to help publicize it from within these torture kamps as well.

I can see how a prisoners' fund can do well to get *Liberation* into the hands of more prisoners across Amerika, these newspapers often give a perspective that most prisoners have never heard, even in the SHU. I find many who have lived a lifetime believing "real" news comes from the corporate media, so the independent press is perhaps the best thing to touch a prisoner's life at this stage.

Well I have more good news, the prison has allowed those of us taking college courses to take three courses per semester now, so now I'm taking three courses, which will help me obtain my degree a lot faster.

I have also been grappling with folks about the so-called "p[rison] i[ndustrial]c[complex]" so I wanted to share my thoughts with you on this.

Any phenomenon which relies on oppression will attract interest in the people who seek to transform society. This interest will generate revolutionary theory that comes at this phenomenon from all perspectives and different peoples. In Amerika today there is a mass criminalization going on in which huge swaths of the population of oppressed people are lassoed from childhood and thus tethered to the prison system for the rest of their lives.

Prisons and the criminal injustice system has reached horrific proportions and with such magnitude of devastation on the people, unseen since the days of slavery. At the same time this devastation unleashed on the people has led some in the quest to identify what is occurring in imperialist Amerika and analyze this onslaught to erroneously label what is occurring as the "prison industrial complex"

Having spent the majority of my life on earth imprisoned I understand all too well what it actually means to be shackled to the state since before puberty, having been on probation or parole since age 11, a ward of the court at 15, from juvenile hall to California Youth Authority, to prison and SHUs. I have lived under the bald repression of the state apparatus for decades. This has led me to engage in a deep study of the mass criminalization that is taking place in Amerika and perhaps to add to this conversation with a perspective derived from the inner core of this mass criminalization which affects millions of people in Amerika.

What is behind this mass criminalization is not a PIC, rather what we are experiencing in Amerika is national oppression! Those who suffer from national oppression in Amerika are the Chicanos, Blacks, Boriquas, First Nations and other who are not hunted and captured on the street in order to exploit our labor and profit off our work or imprisonment, we are captured and imprisoned as a form of social control and to confine the rebellious segments of the oppressed population. Prisons today work to uphold white supremacy by decimating the oppressed in their efforts to organize, by liquidating our leadership and attempting to smother our ability to acquire self determination and thus seize power.

Profit is not at the helm in mass criminalization. In all my years of incarceration I have had two jobs, once as a porter (janitor) and another time in the kitchen. Each job lasted around two months, so when you add up decades of feeding me, housing me, providing me with electricity, clothes, water and free medical care, they have lost profit in my incarceration and my case is more of the norm.

The idea of prison incarceration being profit based comes from those who do not understand imprisonment. Most who propose the PIC idea believe all able bodies in prison work thus making supposed profit but this is just not true. Sadly many in prison want to work, and are instead placed on waiting lists that take years because there are only so many jobs for each yard: We are talking about 50 jobs for a 1,000-man yard and these jobs are not "prison industries" they are porters, kitchen workers, clerks or landscape. Furthermore not all prisons have industries and those that do are mostly to produce items for re use for prisons, i.e., prison clothing, milk, prison shoes, prison eye glasses, etc.

There are those rare instances when a corporation will hook up with a low level prison in order to have prisoners manufacture items but when this happens we are talking less than a hundred prisoners out of thousands and then some prisoners will earn around $4 an hour not 11 cents. California leads Amerika in its prison boom, there are more prisons in California than anywhere else in Amerika but most are state prisons. Only a few of the 30 + prisons are "private prisons" and even then the few private prisons are for those doing a few months for petty nonviolent crimes.

The theft of Mexican land and subsequent terrorized Chicano people, the theft of Africans and the slave trade that followed, the genocide of First Nations and colonization of Boriqua among other horrors has not altered this course of oppression. It has merely transformed and become stealth but our existence under the heel of an oppressor nation continues to be the principal contradiction in Amerika.

The myth of some PIC is quickly dispelled when we learn that the state actually loses money in running prisons. The idea of an invasion of private prisons is simply untrue when we look at the data which shows that over 90 percent of Amerika's prisons are state controlled.

What seems to confuse many is to learn that Amerika holds the most prisoners in the world and being a capitalist based system many naturally believe profit must be the reason. In this case it is national oppression that enables the capitalist system to continue to survive, not profit per se.

I see it as a lion in the wild taking down a water buffalo, in this case U.S. Imperialism being the lion who feeds on some of the carcass and leaves. Then come the hyenas, vultures and rodents, who in this case would be the phone companies, prison guards union, corporations, etc. who feed off the rest but initially the lion did not take down the water buffalo for the other scavengers, rather they benefited after the fact.

Many who promote the idea of a PIC have no problem with imprisoning oppressed people so long as a prisoner's labor is not exploited. This backward thinking will never lead to national liberation. Real national liberation arrives when we build our independent institutions, build public opinion and prepare the grounds for socialist revolution!

The comrades here in Pelican Bay SHU who are studying the mass criminalization in Amerika see those pushing the PIC line as suspect because ultimately those pushing the PIC myth ultimately help imperialism continue its work by not finding ways to combat the real causes of our oppression. Prison industries are not even 1 percent of the gross domestic product so where the hell is the profit motive for Amerika?

Those studying the mass criminalization today in Amerika should also understand the social conditions of prisoners within these dungeon. After all, the whole purpose of learning about a phenomenon is to then transform it in the interests of the people and the future revolution. Our job then as revolutionaries within prisons or out in society should first identify the contradictions surrounding prisons in general and the prison movement in particular. Without this identification a vanguard is unable to apply the proper tactics necessary to move the struggle in a forward motion with regard to prisons today.

The tool we use to make our analysis is dialectical materialism which is, as Marx taught, the way in which we study history and the contradictions in the material world. The principal contradiction within the U.S. prison system is between prisoners vs. the state. But within U.S. prisons also exists the prison movement which is an exclusive phenomenon which has different contradictions. The prison movement is prisoners, ex-prisoners and their allies who work within or around prison issues, i.e., prisoners rights, better conditions and developing a progressive current that can transform into an anti-imperialist prison movement.

The principal contradiction within the prison movement is bourgeois ideology vs. revolutionary ideology. The prison movement like all phenomenon ebbs and flows, develops and retreats, exists in a quantitative stage and at certain junctures makes a leap into a qualitative stage and at times reverts back to a quantitative stage.

The prison movement reached a level where it made a leap as Engles put it "from quantity to quality" in the 1970s with prisoners becoming politicized. This was reflected most notably with George Jackson and events surrounding this time period, with the San Quentin Six, Attica and many other events which demonstrated prisoners who came to identify their national oppression and no longer saw other poor prisoners as the threat. Rather they correctly observed the state as their oppressor and rose up in accordance to this realization.

What was occurring on the streets in the struggles for national liberation was interconnected to the struggles of prisoners. In this way oppressed people out in society as well as in prisons were able to draw on each others' victories and determination in the common path forward.

When COINTELPRO was unleashed it not only devastated the peoples struggles out in society but the prison movement as well and so during the 1980s the prison movement reverted back into quantitative change and was so for decades, until now.

Today we are seeing prisons once more making that leap into qualitative change. This is reflected in the many prison protests going on across Amerika, particularly the 2011 hunger strikes that were spearheaded by prisoners in Pelican Bay SHU which at its peak included over 12,000 prisoners across Amerika.

Due to the state not meeting the five demands initially proposed in 2011 a new round of strikes is set for July 8th which is expected to be the largest prison strike in U.S. history, providing thus more evidence of qualitative change, the "call to end hostilities" between different nationalities in California which also came out of Pelican Bay SHU speaks further to prisoners realizing we represent a class within prisons and identifying the contradiction we face as an oppressed class.

In coming to understand the principal contradiction within the prison movement it becomes possible to find ways to resolve this contradiction where some may want to be bribed by the state with items we don't currently have and those who want substantial change and the ability to better operate and build independent institutions within prisons in order to politicize these dungeons from the inside out. Mao wrote in his piece "on contradiction" that "The nature of a thing is determined mainly by the principal aspect of a contradiction, the aspect which has gained the dominant position."

The prison movement today grapples with this internal contradiction as well where many are working to steer these efforts to a more revolutionary path, where the revolutionary ideology as Mao put it "has gained the dominant position."

Most recently the state has begun to use the control unit, whether they are called SHU, SMU or any other name in order to refine the use of prisons to better inflict national oppression. The use of solitary confinement is the current weapon of choice which the state is using, in what will in the future result in the state rendering— purposely—the largest population of mentally ill in perhaps world history. There are thousands currently in solitary confinement with many more having left the SHU after years of torture only to leave mentally ill. This new weapon of choice is used on select people who have resisted the state but whose main violation is thought crimes in which no physical acts are done, rather one's ideology is the main factor that threatens the state.

Prisoners today understand that poor people in prisons across Amerika are suffering just like their counterparts in other prisons and that ultimately we will not overcome torture and abuse lest we come together as a class with class interests.

I call on all prisoners in prisons across Amerika to end the hostilities and form a united front in response to the oppression we all face as prisoners, rebuild that revolutionary spirit which propelled prior generations in these very cages to rise above our circumstances and identify the real oppressor! Reclaim your humanity even from within these concentration camps and let us march in sync on our long march to liberation. What we must do is raise consciousness in these concentration camps and unmask the brutality we face in Amerika. As Comrade Che said "The blood of the people is our most sacred treasure, but it must be used in order to save the blood of more people in the future" (Tactics and Strategy of the Latin American Revolution).

We understand that in order to save others from suffering this torture, this madness in SHU, we must struggle, we must resist our oppressor lest this oppression continue!

La Lucha Sigue! The struggle continues!
Jose H. Villarreal

P.S. Brother Ben, I would like to read an analysis on the Soviet Union's first five year plan. I know it pulled them out of debt. I also want to read the PSL line on the Chicano nation. I appreciate your assistance. Also enclosed is 1-poem and 1-picture of myself. Also I'm working on a drawing for you all.

Endnotes

Chapter One: An overview of mass incarceration

1   The last year from which we could find a comprehensive world-wide list of male incarceration rates was 2006, at which point 736 out of 100,000 white men were incarcerated. That would place the incarceration rate of white men 11th among men in 178 listed countries. These rates were drawn from the Status of Men Index, 2009 (see http://www.vcclan.org/forums/view.php?pg = someni_male_incarcerations) based on statistics provided by Roy Walmsley's annual "World Prison Population List" (International Centre for Prison Studies).

2   Justice Policy Institute, "The Punishing Decade: Prison and Jail Estimates at the Millenium." May 2000, p.1.

3   Bureau of Justice, "State and Federal Prisoners, 1925-1985" (Oct. 1986) p.2

4   Lauren E. Glaze, "Correctional Population in the United States, 2010." (Bureau of Justice, 2010)

5   Paul Guerino, Paige M. Harrison and William J. Sabol, "Prisoners in 2010," (Bureau of Justice, 2010); Glazer, 2010

6   1,446,000 men are in state and federal prison, while 104,600 women are under the control of the same correctional authorities.

7   Glaze, "Correctional Population," Appendix Table 3, p. 8. Accessed Sept. 10, 2012 at http://www.bjs.gov/content/pub/pdf/cpus10.pdf.

8   Paul Guerino, Paige M. Harrison, and William J. Sabol, "Prisoners in 2010," Appendix Table 14. Accessed Sept. 10, 2012 at http://bjs.ojp.usdoj.gov/content/pub/pdf/p10.pdf

9   Heather Ann Thompson, "Why Mass Incarceration Matters," Journal of American History (December 2010); Paul Guerino,

Paige M. Harrison and William J. Sabol, "Prisoners in 2010," (Bureau of Justice, 2010); National Institute on Drug Abuse, "Drug Use Among Racial/Ethnic Minorities," (NIH, 1998)

10 http://www.hrw.org/news/2009/09/22/mental-illness-human-rights-and-us-prisons

11 Doris J. James and Lauren Glaze, Mental Health Problems of Prison and Jail Inmates (Bureau of Justice, Washington 2006)

12 http://www.hrw.org/node/12252/section/4

13 http://afsc.org/sites/afsc.civicactions.net/files/documents/ Buried Alive.pdf, p.18

14 Bruce Western, Vincent Schiraldi and Jason Ziedenberg, "Education & Incarceration," (Justice Policy Institute, August 2003)

15 Advancement Project, "Education on Lockdown: The Schoolhouse to Jailhouse Track," (March 2005)

16 http://www.aclu.org/racial-justice/school-prison-pipeline-talking-points

17 Advancement Project, 2005

18 Greg Blustein, "Corrections Firm Offers States Cash for Prisons," Associated Press March 9, 2012

19 "Kids-for-cash financier Powell assigned to Fla. prison camp," December 28, 2011, Scranton Times Tribune

20 Cody Mason, Too Good To Be True: Private Prisons in America," (The Sentencing Project, January 2012)

21 Justice Policy Institute, Gaming the System: How Political Strategies of Private Prison Companies Promote Ineffective Incarceration Policies (June 2011)

22 Detention Watch Network, "The Influence of the Private Prison Industry in Immigration Detention," http://www.detentionwatch-network.org/privateprisons

23 Laura Sullivan, "Prison Economics Help Drive Ariz. Immigration Law" NPR Radio (October 28, 2010) http://www.npr. org/2010/10/28/130833741/prison-economics-help-drive-ariz-im-migration-law

24 Ibid.

25 Ibid.

26 Richard A. Oppel Jr., "Private Prisons Found to Offer Little in Savings," New York Times (May 18, 2011); Arizona Department

of Corrections, "FY 2010 Operating Per Capita Cost Report," (April 13, 20110

27 Associated Press, "New Mexico Pays More for Private Prisons, Report Says," (May 24, 2007)

28 This a reference to the "Abt" and "BOP" reports, initiated by the National Institute of Justice. http://www.nij.gov/journals/259/prison-privatization.htm; McDonald, D.C., and K. Carlson, Contracting for Imprisonment in the Federal Prison System: Cost and Performance of the Privately Operated Taft Correctional Institution, final report submitted to the National Institute of Justice, November 2005 (NCJ 211990); Camp, S.D., and D.M. Daggett, Evaluation of the Taft Demonstration Project: Performance of a Private-Sector Prison and the BOP, Washington, DC: Federal Bureau of Prisons, October 2005; Nelson, J., Competition in Corrections: Comparing Public and Private Sector Operations, Alexandria, VA: The CNA Corporation, December 2005.

29 Oppel, "Private Prisons Found to Offer Little in Savings," New York Times (May 18, 2011)

30 Ibid.

31 http://www.kitescampaigns.org/images/campaigns/PLN-telephone-article-4-7-11.pdf, pp.1-3

32 http://www.bop.gov/inmate_programs/work_prgms.jsp

33 http://www.nytimes.com/2012/03/15/business/private-businesses-fight-federal-prisons-for-contracts.html?pagewanted = all

34 http://www.thenation.com/article/162478/hidden-history-alec-and-prison-labor

35 "Frequently Asked Questions (FAQs) about Procurement at the City of New York," http://www1.ccny.cuny.edu/facultystaff/financeadmin/upload/FAQs-on-Purchasing.pdf

36 Doug Hornig, "The Perils of Prison Labor," Businessweek (March 19, 2001) http://www.businessweek.com/magazine/content/01_12/b3724136.htm

37 Frederick W. Derrick, Charles E. Scott and Thomas Hutson, "Prison Labor Effects on the Unskilled Labor Market," The American Economist (Fall 2004)

Chapter Two: Enter the torture chambers

1   Guerino, Paul; Harrison, Paige M.; and Sabol, William J., "Prisoners in 2010," Bureau of Justice Statistics, (Washington, DC: US Department of Justice, December 2011), NCJ 236096, p. 7. http://bjs.ojp.usdoj.gov/content/pub/pdf/p10.pdf

2   http://www.nytimes.com/2008/05/20/nyregion/20prisons.html

3   http://www.illinoistimes.com/Springfield/article-7025-illinois-prisons-standing-room-only.html

4   Ibid.

5   Ibid.

6   http://www.huffingtonpost.com/2011/09/28/illinois-prison-overcrowd_n_985410.html

7   http://www.alec.org/initiatives/prison-overcrowding/prison-overcrowding-kentucky/; http://www.pewcenteronthestates.org/initiatives_detail.aspx?initiativeID=56236

8   http://www.alabamapolicy.org/standanddeliver/article.php?IDArticle=81

9   http://smartoncrimema.org/cost-of-prison-over-crowding/factsheets/

10 http://www.radioiowa.com/2011/04/12/iowa-prison-population-tops-9000/

11 http://motherjones.com/politics/2008/07/convicting-california

12 http://www.lao.ca.gov/reports/2011/crim/overcrowding_080511.aspx

13 http://www.usatoday.com/news/washington/judicial/2011-05-24-Supreme-court-prisons_n.htm

14 http://motherjones.com/politics/2008/07/convicting-california.p.2

15 http://www.tribune-chronicle.com/page/content.detail/id/145808/Ohio-1st-in-US-to-sell-prison-to-private-company-.html

16 http://www.nccourts.org/Courts/CRS/Councils/spac/Documents/2011-popproj.pdf

17 Ibid.

18 http://www.prisonpolicy.org/prisonindex/behindthewalls.html

19 https://www.prisonlegalnews.org/

20 Patrick Howe, "Cost Cutters Slash Prison Food Budgets," CBS,

May 2003 (http://www.cbsnews.com/stories/2003/05/14/politics/main553785.shtml)

21 Ibid.

22 Ibid.

23 "Cold Breakfast on the Menu for Linn County Inmates," ABC 9 News, http://kezi.com/page/106106

24 "Lawmaker asks attorney general to investigate Aramark's prison food contract," Kentucky.com, http://www.kentucky.com/2011/01/10/1593198/lawmaker-asks-attorney-general.html

25 "Kentucky prison inmates don't like the food, and it shows," McClatchy DC, http://www.mcclatchydc.com/2009/10/21/77553/kentucky-prison-inmates-dont-like.html

26 Valerie Honeycutt-Spears, "Audit: State Overpays by Thousands of Dollars on Prison Food Contract," Lexington Herald-Leader October 8, 2010; John Cheves, "Lawmaker Asks Attorney General to Investigate Aramark's Prison Food Contract," Lexington Herald-Leader January 10, 2011

27 Alex Leary, "Inmates Say Prison Food Made Them Sick," Tampa Bay Times May 13, 2008; https://www.prisonlegalnews.org/displayArticle.aspx?articleid = 22246

28 Ibid.

29 Ibid.

30 Ibid.

31 http://www.doc.state.mn.us/publications/documents/11-11MN-PrisonVisitationStudy.pdf

32 http://afsc.org/sites/afsc.civicactions.net/files/documents/Buried Alive.pdf, p. 8

33 Ibid.

34 http://www.huffingtonpost.com/2011/11/28/solitary-confinement-colorado-prisoners_n_1117433.html; http://www.guardian.co.uk/commentisfree/cifamerica/2011/oct/17/california-prisoners-hunger-strike

35 http://www.solitaryconfinement.org/uploads/sourcebook_web.pdf, p.10

36 http://www.cpt.coe.int/en/annual/rep-21.pdf, p.43

37 http://www.solitaryconfinement.org/uploads/sourcebook_web.pdf, p.11

38 Ibid.

39 Ibid.
40 http://afsc.org/sites/afsc.civicactions.net/files/documents/
    PrisonInsideThePrison.pdf. p. 16
41 http://www.solitaryconfinement.org/uploads/sourcebook_web.
    pdf, p.21
42 Ibid.
43 http://afsc.org/sites/afsc.civicactions.net/files/documents/
    Buried Alive.pdf, p.6
44 http://www.hrw.org/node/12252/section/19
45 http://afsc.org/sites/afsc.civicactions.net/files/documents/
    Buried Alive.pdf, p. 18
46 http://www.washingtonpost.com/local/dc-politics/va-pris-
    ons-use-of-solitary-confinement-is-scrutinized/2011/11/28/gIQA-
    kKHuhP_story.html
47 Ibid.
48 http://www.hrw.org/node/12252/section/19
49 http://www.afsc.org/sites/afsc.civicactions.net/files/documents/
    Buried Alive PMRO May08.pdf, p.7
50 Ibid, p.8
51 http://afsc.org/sites/afsc.civicactions.net/files/documents/
    Buried Alive.pdf, p.26
52 Ibid.
53 Ibid.
54 Ibid.
55 Ibid.
56 American Psychiatric Association, Psychiatric Services in Jails
    and Prisons, 2nd Ed. (Washington D.C., American Psychiatric
    Association, 2000), p. 6. (as quoted in HRW report)
57 State of Washington Department of Corrections Final Report
    Health Care Facility Master Plan, DLR Group in association with
    Pulitzer/Bogard & Associates, L.L.C., 2000 (as quoted in hrw
    report)
58 http://www.hrw.org/node/12252/section/15
59 Ibid.
60 Ibid.
61 http://www.clearinghouse.net/chDocs/public/PC-AL-0013-0002.
    pdf
62 http://www.washingtonpost.com/local/dc-politics/va-pris-

ons-use-of-solitary-confinement-is-scrutinized/2011/11/28/gIQA-kKHuhP_story.html

63 http://www.ihep.org/assets/files/publications/g-l/LearningReduceRecidivism.pdf, p.16

64 http://www.bop.gov/news/research_projects/published_reports/recidivism/orepredprg.pdf, p. 10

65 http://www.ceanational.org/PDFs/EdReducesCrime.pdf, p. 12

66 http://www.ceanational.org/PDFs/EdReducesCrime.pdf, p. 10; http://www.bop.gov/news/research_projects/published_reports/recidivism/orepredprg.pdf, p. 10

67 http://www.ihep.org/assets/files/publications/g-l/LearningReduceRecidivism.pdf, p. 14

68 San Francisco Chronicle Februarry 16, 2010, by Maria Lagos, "Cuts In Programs To Help Inmates Questioned."

Chapter Three: The history of US incarceration

1 Matthew W. Meskell, "An American Resolution: The History of Prisons in the United States 1777-1877," Stanford Law Review (April 1999); Nicole Hahn Rafter, "Prisons for Women, 1790-1980," Crime and Justice (Vol. 5 1983)

2 Matthew W. Meskell, "An American Resolution;" Rafter, "Prisons for Women."

3 Rafter, "Prisons for Women," p. 135

4 Matthew W. Meskell, "An American Resolution;" Rafter, "Prisons for Women."

5 Edward L. Ayers, Vengence and Justice: Crime and Punishment in the Ninteenth Century American South (Oxford, London 1985) p. 212 as quoted in Gavin Wright, "Convict Labor After Emancipation: Old or New South?" Georgia Historical Quarterly (Summer 1997)

6 Wright, "Convict Labor," p.455

7 Matthew J. Mancini, "Race, Economics, and The Abandonment of Convict Leasing" Journal of Negro History (Oct. 1978) p. 341

Chapter Four: Revolution in the air

1 John Lewis, Walking With the Wind (Harcourt and Brace, New York 1998) p.219

2   Violence in the City—An End or a Beginning?: A Report By the Governors Commission on the Los Angeles Riots, 1965

3   Report of The National Advisory Commission on Civil Disorders (1968) p. 5

4   Ibid.

5   Joe R. Feagin and Harlan Hahn, Ghetto Revolts: The Politics of Violence in American Cities (Macmillian, New York 1973) p. 268

6   Ibid, p. 269

7   Ibid, p. 4

8   Susan Welch, "The Impact of Urban Riots on Urban Expenditures," American Journal of Political Science (Nov. 1975) p.743

9   Feagin and Hahn, "Ghetto Revolts," pp. 101-108

10 Feagin and Hahn, "Ghetto Revolts," p. 102

11 Col. Robert D. Heinl Jr., "Collapse of the Armed Forces" Armed Forces Journal (June, 1971)

12 David Cortright, Soldiers in Revolt (Haymarket, Chicago 2005) p.3

13 Ibid.

14 Ibid, p.10

15 Heinl, "Are Z-Grams Backfiring?" p.29

16 Heinl, "Collapse of the Armed Forces"

17 Ibid.

18 Cortright, "Soldiers," p.5

19 Ibid.

20 Heinl, "Collapse of the Armed Forces"

21 Ibid.

22 Terry H. Anderson, "The Movement and the Sixties" Oxford University Press, 1995.

Chapter Five: The law-and-order response

1   "The Republican Assault on the Senate," Time Magazine (October 26, 1970)

2   Ibid.

3   Alexander Bickel, "Crime, The Courts, and the Old Nixon," The New Republic (June 15, 1968), p.9

4   Ibid, p.8

5   Charles E. Jones, "The Political Repression of the Black Panther Party," Journal of Black Studies (June, 1988) p.416

6   Mumia Abu-Jamal, We Want Freedom: A Life in the Black Panther Party, (SouthEnd, Cambridge 2004) p. 122

7   Newsweek, 1969. As quoted in: Mumia Abu-Jamal, We Want Freedom: A Life in the Black Panther Party, (South End, Cambridge 2004) p. 117

8   Abu-Jamal, "We Want Freedom," p. 272

9   Ibid, p. 121

10 Bobby Seale, Seize The Time, (Vintage, New York 1968) p. 180

11 David Garrow, "FBI Political Harassment and FBI Historiography: Analyzing Informants and Measuring the Effects," The Public Historian (Autumn, 1988) p. 9

12 Henry Louis Gates interview of Eldridge Cleaver, Frontline (http://www.pbs.org/wgbh/pages/frontline/shows/race/interviews/ecleaver.html)

13 Charles E. Jones, "The Political Repression of the Black Panther Party 1966-1971: The Case of the Oakland Bay Area," Journal of Black Studies (June, 1988) p. 424

14 Gerard J. De Groot, "Ronald Reagan and Student Unrest in California: 1966-1970," Pacific Historical Review (Feb. 1996) pp. 115-116

15 Adam Winkler, "The Secret History of Guns," Atlantic Magazine (September 2011) p.2

16 De Groot, pp. 116-117

17 Time noted Rizzo's "crisis" management skills were not-so-thinly veiled language about "blacks, crime and drugs." "A Tough Cop for Mayor," Time Magazine (May 31, 1971); Steve Neal, "Attilla the Cop," The Nation (October 30, 1976) .

18 Steve Neal, "Attilla the Cop," The Nation (October 30, 1976) p.425

19 "Ousting a Reformer," Time Magazine (December 20, 1971)

20 Anthony M. Platt, "The Politics of Law and Order, Social Justice (Fall 1994) p. 6

21 "Street Crime: Who's Winning?" Time Magazine (October 23, 1972)

22 Gene Gilmore, "One Year of Frank Rizzo," (December 25, 1972) p.659

23 Robert F. Diegelmann "Federal Financial Assistance for Crime

Control Lessons from the Leaa Experience," Journal of Criminal Law & Criminology (Fall 1982)

24 Peter B. Kraska and Derek J. Paulson, "Grounded Research into US Paramilitary Policing," Policing and Society (February 1997) p. 254

25 Matthew Fleischer, "Policing Revolution," Los Angeles Times Magazine (April, 2011)

Chapter Six: Economic and ideological restructuring

1 http://inflationdata.com/inflation/inflation_rate/historicalinflation.aspx

2 "Recovery in a Deep Freeze," Time Magazine (Feb. 7, 1977)

3 Arthur M. Okun, "The Great Stagflation Swamp," Challenge (November/December 1977) p.9

4 R. Jeffery Lustig, "The Politics of Shutdown: Community, Property, and Corporatism," Journal of Economic Problems (March 1985) p. 128

5 "Detroit Bucks a Buyers Rebellion," Time Magazine (Dec. 2, 1974)

6 Paul W. McCracken, "Economic Policy in the Nixon Years," Presidential Studies Quarterly (Winter, 1996) pp.167-168

7 Phillip Foner, Organized Labor and the Black Worker 1619-1981, (International Publishers, New York 1981) pp. 425-429

8 http://www.bls.gov/cps/cpsrace2010.pdf, p.9

9 Robert Carbaugh and John Olienyk, "US Steelmakers in Continuing Crisis," Challenge (January-February 2004, pp. 88-92.

10 Thomas Sowell, Civil Rights: Rhetoric or Reality, (Basic Books, New York 1984) pp. 19-20

11 William Julius Wilson, "The Underclass: Issues, Perspectives, and Public Policy," Annals of the American Academy of Political and Social Science (Jan 1989) p. 183

12 William Julius Wilson, "The Plight of the Inner-City Black Male," Proceedings of the American Philosophical Society (September, 1993) p. 324

13 Herbert Hill, "Racial Inequality in Employment: The Patterns of Discrimination," Annals of the American Academy of Political and Social Science (Jan. 1965)

14 Cited in Herbert Hill, "Employment, Manpower Training, and the Black Worker," (Summer, 1969)

15 Phillip Foner, Organized Labor and the Black Worker 1619-1981, (International Publishers, New York 1981) p.398

16 Christopher L. Foote, Warren C. Whatley and Gavin Wright, "Arbitraging a Discriminatory Labor Market: Black Workers at the Ford Motor Company, 1918–1947," Journal of Labor Economics (July, 2003)

17 Michael B. Katz and Mark J. Stern, "Beyond Discrimination: Understanding African-American Inequality in the 21st Century," Dissent (Winter 2008)

18 Michael B. Katz, Mark J. Stern and Jaime J. Fader, "The New African American Inequality," Journal of American History (June 2005)

19 Margaret Zumido and Michael I. Lichter, "Bad Attitudes and Good Soldiers: Soft Skills as a Code for Tractability in the Hiring of Immigrant Latina/os over Native Blacks in the Hotel Industry" Social Problems (Nov. 2008)

20 Ibid.

21 Hill, 1965

22 Foner, p. 341

Chapter Seven: The 'war on drugs'

1 James R. Thompson, "Foreword: Remarks by James Thompson," Northwestern School of Law Journal of Criminal Law and Sociology (Fall 1982)

2 Anthony M. Platt, "The Politics of Law and Order," Social Justice (Fall 1994) p. 8

3 http://www.prisonpolicy.org/scans/bjs/cpus10.pdf, p. 1

4 http://www.sentencingproject.org/doc/publications/publications/inc_noexitseptember2009.pdf, p. 7

5 Platt, "The Politics of Law and Order," p. 8

6 Steven A. Holmes, "The Boom in Jails is Locking up Lots of Loot," New York Times (November 6, 1994)

7 Holmes, "The Boom in Jails,"

8 John J. Dilulio, "Targeting Inner-Cities: The Next War on Drugs," Brookings Review (Summer of 1993) p. 28

9 Barton Gellman and Elsa Walsh, "D.C. Gets Tougher Drug Laws;

Emergency Measure May Jam Courts," Washington Post (August 2, 1989)

10 Alfonso A. Narvaez, "As Prison Opens in Jersey, Officials Support Bond Issue," New York Times (Oct. 21, 1987)

11 Ibid.

12 http://carnegieendowment.org/pdf/files/mgi-ch3.pdf

13 Ibid.

14 http://www.unodc.org/documents/data-and-analysis/Studies/ Illicit_financial_flows_2011_web.pdf, p. 21

15 http://www.abtassociates.com/reports/american_users_ spend_2002.pdf, p.3

16 Ibid.

17 http://money.cnn.com/magazines/fortune/fortune500/2012/ full_list/

18 Stephanie Coontz, The Way We Never Were: American Families and the Nostalgia Trap (New York, Basic 1992) pp. 247-248

19 Joel Brinkley, "Drug Law Raises More than Hope," New York Times (Nov. 2, 1986)

20 Charles Rangel, "We Need a Coordinated National Drug Policy," New York Times (September 18, 1987)

21 http://www.ussc.gov/Legislative_and_Public_Affairs/ Congressional_Testimony_and_Reports/Mandatory_Minimum_ Penalties/20111031_RtC_PDF/Chapter_02.pdf

22 Bernard Weinraub, "Reagan Call for Cut in Drug Fight Ignites the Anger of Both Parties," New York Times (January 8, 1987)

23 Jon F. Hale, "The Making of the New Democrats," Political Science Quarterly (Summer 1995) p. 220

24 Larry Rohter, "In Wave of Anti-Crime Fervor, States Rush to Adopt Laws," New York Times (May 10, 1994)

25 William Claibourne, "State Legislators Rethink '3 Strikes' Laws as Costs Begin at Home," Washington Post (August 7, 1994)

26 Larry Rohter, "In Wave of Anti-Crime Fervor, States Rush to Adopt Laws," New York Times (May 10, 1994)

27 It is very notable that in a 1993 speech at a Black church in Memphis where Clinton spoke about crime, and ghetto conditions, he cited William Julius Wilson's research in particular, even using some of the same buzzwords. This would be an enduring element of the Clinton Administration, where policy

makers would cite Wilson's work as central to the understanding of urban issues that underlay their neoliberal social policy.

28 Nancy Gibbs and James Carney, "Laying Down the Law," TIME (August, 23, 1993)

29 The Editors, "Mr. Guiliani's Energetic First Year," New York Times (January 3, 1995)

30 Joseph B. Treaster, "Local Reaction to Crime Bill: Delight, with some Doubts," New York Times (September 14, 1994)

31 Marianne Yen, "Aftershock; Boot Camp System for Youthful Offenders is Taking a Crack at Crime. But How Effective Is it?" Washington Post (Nov. 20, 1994)

32 Ibid.

33 Ibid.

34 In fairness the CBC did offer opposition to aspects of the 1994 Crime Bill initiated by Clinton. Then mostly all voted for it.

35 Michael A. Fletcher, "Low-Profile Year 'Extremely Productive' for NAACP, Mfume Says," Washington Post February 16, 1997

36 Sam Walker, "Black Churches in America Battle Another Foe: Inertia," Christian Science Monitor July 5, 1996to the Secretary on the Acquiescence of this Government in the Murder of the Jews," Jan. 13, 1944.

Chapter Eight: Debunking bourgeois theories of 'crime'

1 Nathan Glazer, "On subway graffiti in New York," Public Interest (Winter, 1979) p. 8

2 Eric D. Gould, Bruce A. Weinberg and David B. Mustard, "Crime Rates and Local Labor Market Opportunities in the United States 1979-1997," The Review of Economics and Statistics (Feb. 2002)

3 Jeffery Fagan and Richard B. Freeman, "Crime and Work," Crime and Justice (Vol. 25 1999), p. 252

4 Ibid, p. 251

5 Ibid, p. 256

6 Stephanie Coontz, The Way We Never Were: American Families and the Nostalgia Trap (New York, Basic 1992) p. 251

7 Ibid, pp. 258-260

8 Marcia Carlson, Sara McLanahan and Jeanne Brooks-Gunn, "Unmarried but Not Absent: Fathers Involvement with Children After A Nonmarital Birth," Marriage and Family Formation

Among Low-Income Couples: What Do We Know From Research Georgetown University Sept. 4-5 2003, Published May 2005

9   Coontz, "The Way We Never Were," p. 247

Chapter Nine: What alternatives to mass incarceration?

1   American Probation and Parole Association, "Position Statement: Conditional Early Release Program," Jan. 1998, Accessed Aug. 30, 2012. http://www.appa-net.org/eweb/Dynamicpage.aspx-?site = APPA_2&webcode = IB_PositionStatement

2   Heather Mac Donald, "It's the Cops Stupid," The New Republic (Feb. 2, 2012)

3   Heather Mac Donald, "Fighting Crime Where the Criminals Are," New York Times (June 25, 2010)

4   In more ways than one.

CONTACT THE PARTY FOR SOCIALISM AND LIBERATION

NATIONAL OFFICES

San Francisco, CA
sf@pslweb.org
2969 Mission St., Suite 200
San Francisco, CA 94110
415-821-6171

Washington, DC
dc@pslweb.org
PO Box 26451
Washington, DC 20001
202-234-2828

BRANCHES

Albuquerque, NM
abq@pslweb.org
505-503-3067

Baltimore MD
baltimore@pslweb.org
443-731-6471

Boston, MA
boston@pslweb.org
857-334-5084

Chicago, IL
chicago@pslweb.org
773-920-7590

Long Beach, CA
lb@pslweb.org

Los Angeles, CA
la@pslweb.org
323-810-3380

Miami, FL
miami@pslweb.org
305-209-2503

New Haven, CT
ct@pslweb.org
203-416-8365

New Paltz, NY
np@pslweb.org

New York City, NY
nyc@pslweb.org
212-694-8762

Philadelphia, PA
philly@pslweb.org
267-281-3859

Pittsburgh, PA
pittsburgh@pslweb.org

Sacramento, CA
sac@pslweb.org

San Diego, CA
sandiego@pslweb.org
619-508-6756

San José, CA
sanjose@pslweb.org
408-829-9507

Santa Cruz, CA
santacruz@pslweb.org

Seattle, WA
seattle@pslweb.org
206-367-3820

Syracuse, NY
syracuse@pslweb.org

for a complete listing visit PSLweb.org